# From Man to Woman

*The Transgender Journey
of
Virginia Prince*

# From Man to Woman
## *The Transgender Journey*
## *of Virginia Prince*

RICHARD F. DOCTER

Professor of Psychology (Emeritus)
Department of Psychology, California State University
Northridge, California
91330-8255

Affiliated Scholar
Center for Feminist Research
University of Southern California

*DocPress@aol.com*
*Docter Press: Northridge, CA*
*P.O. Box 280126 Northridge, CA 91328-0126*

ISBN 0-9745600-0-6

Transsexualism -- United States -- History
Transvestism -- United States -- History
Transgender -- United States -- History

Printed in the United States of America

# Acknowledgments

I met Virginia Prince in 1979 at California State University, Northridge, where I have been a Professor of Psychology since 1966. She had been invited to speak to an evening class led by my colleague, Dr. Richard Smith. Over time, Prince and I became friends and we met often at transgender events or at her home. For the past decade I have shared ideas with Virginia, and obtained from her a more detailed record of her life. The writing of this biography came into focus when Vern Bullough, distinguished sex researcher and historian, urged me to proceed with the project. Vern's wife, Bonnie Bullough, who died in 1996, also knew Virginia well and over several years she kindly had shared with me some interesting stories about Ms. Prince. I also owe my thanks to several of the early members of the original Alpha Chapter, all of whom respect Virginia's considerable achievements.

Jane Fee helped me by taking time to review the organizational skills and leadership abilities of Prince. Irene Ellis, a long-time friend of Virginia's, also gave generously of her time and has donated historical materials to the CSUN Libraries. Publisher Sandy Thomas knows Virginia well, and over the years we have often shared thoughts about her contributions and her human relationships.

Tony Gardner is the Special Collections Librarian at California State University, Northridge. He has been very helpful in pointing out various Prince materials used in this biography. I am also much indebted to a friend of many years, Valdis Volkovskis, who spent many hours helping me with a variety of computer problems and by reproducing and scanning most of the pictures in this book.

Two well-known gender counselors and authors have been exceptionally helpful by providing a thoughtful reading of the manuscript and by offering numerous suggestions for improvement: I refer to Janis Walworth and Niela Miller, each of whom gave me invaluable help, both by taking a broad overview of my effort, and also by pointing out factual errors. I owe them special thanks for their many excellent ideas and editorial suggestions. Janis has also helped to educate me concerning the facts of life about the self-publication of a book.

I am most appreciative to Alison and Dottie Laing, along with Joan Hoff and Denise LeClair at IFGE, Sandra Cole, Maureen Osborne, Sister Mary Elizabeth, and many others within the transgender community, who provided their points of view about their friend, Virginia Prince. This includes Rikki Swin who kindly showed me through the collection of Prince materials held at The Rikki Swin Institute in downtown Chicago. Fellow gender researchers Richard Ekins and David King helped me to sort out some troublesome facts. Thank you, all!

One of the greatest contributions to understanding the life of Virginia Prince is the twenty-nine year record of her interviews with Dr. Robert Stoller, a former colleague of mine at UCLA Medical School. He deserves special recognition for the unique record he compiled from 1962 to 1991. Virginia's story could not have been told without the interviews he preserved. I am certain that the Prince-Stoller records offer a unique glimpse into the thinking of both Dr. Stoller and Dr. Prince, and that they may represent one of the most detailed records of research interviews ever to be acquired. I have devoted a chapter to these materials.

Through a succession of drafts, my wife, Shirley Long Docter, has patiently encouraged attention to spelling, punctuation, and grammatical structure, along with important insights into the life of Dr. Prince. Finally, I'd like to thank Virginia for being a very understanding, patient, responsive, and cooperative research subject. At the outset of this effort I cautioned her that an authentic biographical effort was not supposed to be a rose-colored list of her achievements, and she agreed. I hope I have been able to tell the story of her remarkable life with accuracy, balance, and clarity.

*Richard F. Docter*

*(Left) Vern Bullough, Viginia Prince, Richard Docter, Richard Smith*

# Preface

Virginia Prince, aka Charles Prince and Virginia Bruce, and born Arnold Lowman, started a movement. Few people in history can have that said about them. Though probably unknown to most of the world at large, it is largely due to her that transvestites became organized and the phenomenon became defined.

Cross dressers have been known throughout history, and in some societies they even had special roles such as the Hijras in India or the Kabuki actors in Japan. In the western world there were often female impersonators, cross-dressing individuals, some of whom were prostitutes, and even molly clubs where gay men gathered and often dressed as women, but there is no evidence in Western culture of what might be called a heterosexual transvestite consciousness before the twentieth century (Bullough & Bullough, 1993).

The term itself was coined by Magnus Hirschfeld (1910) who presented a series of case studies which were added to by Havelock Ellis (1928). Ellis preferred the term eonism, however, because he felt the phenomenon went beyond cross dressing. Virginia Prince went further. In 1960 she began organizing transvestites, giving them group identity, encouraging them to speak with their own voice. She gave the definitions which were accepted for the most part of the twentieth century and which furnished the original description in the *Diagnostic and Statistical Manual* of the American Psychiatric Association.

Extremely influential in motivating Virginia Prince to become active in defining and distinguishing transvestism was the case of Christine Jorgensen who achieved world wide publicity in 1952 when she declared that she had been changed from a man into a woman by surgeons in Denmark. The subsequent media coverage of Jorgensen helped transsexuals to develop an identity that was supported by the professionals who staffed the newly established gender identity clinics. Initially, at least in the mind of many in the public, including Jorgensen's own surgeon in Denmark, Transsexualism was confused with transvestism (Hamburger et al., 1953). It was Prince who provided what John Gagnon and William Simon (1973) called the sexual script which they felt guided all social activities which transvestites like her (I will use the female pronoun throughout because she has lived as a woman for nearly 40 years) were normal heterosexual men who sought only to express the "woman within." When pressed, however, she would admit that some homosexual transvestites existed, but she excluded them from her definitions of transvestism and, whenever possible, from her groups. She also insisted that transvestism was not an early stage of transsexualism (although in many cases it was). She did not approve of masochism, bondage, sadism, fetishism, or even references to masturbation in the popular fiction she distributed for transvestite readers or in her more scholarly writings. She was conscious of the eroticism involved in cross dressing but was reluctant to discuss the sexual elements. She also argued that only men should be considered transvestites because their roles were so restricted they needed to cross dress; women, on the other hand, could not only wear any kind of clothes they wanted but could also express a wider range of emotions so they had no need to be transvestites.

x

As Prince developed her ideas, she managed to organize, publicize, and indoctrinate others about what she felt were the parameters of transvestism. Traveling widely, she established contacts which often developed into clubs and allowed transvestites to identify themselves and to learn how, in her terms, "to express the girl or the woman within." She established a publishing house that disseminated information world wide; she traveled and made public appearances and for many years served as a role model for many transvestites. For twenty years or more she was the dominant voice of transvestism, although increasingly there were individuals who disagreed with her interpretation, and some went their own way. It was only in the 1980s, however, when she was past the age of retirement, that others effectively challenged her leadership of the movement, and put forth different interpretations, but even those who disagreed with her continue to recognize her contributions as the pioneer of the growing transvestite movement.

In short she is a person who deserves a biography and this is just what Richard Docter has done so well. He puts Virginia into context, and gives the reader a very real understanding of who she was and is and what she accomplished, no easy task because Virginia, though cooperative, remains reluctant to reveal too much of herself, and sometimes seems to have forgotten when and what occurred. What appears from the biography is a determined and often dogmatic person, not afraid of expressing her views, determined to expand awareness of transvestism, and devoting her life to the cause, but then this is what it takes to establish a movement.

*Vern L. Bullough, Ph.D., R.N.*

# Contents

| CHAPTER | | PAGE |
|---|---|---|
| 1 | Introduction | 5 |
| 2 | The Lowman Family | 9 |
| 3 | Education | 25 |
| 4 | Two Marriages | 31 |
| 5 | Cross Dressing Era | 43 |
| 6 | Transgender Era | 55 |
| 7 | Prince-Stoller Interviews | 63 |
| 8 | Transvestia Magazine | 75 |
| 9 | Revolt of the Alpha Chapter | 87 |
| 10 | Organizations and Leaders | 91 |
| 11 | The Girl Within | 99 |
| 12 | Battles: Postal Authorities | 111 |
| 13 | Three Motivational Themes | 117 |
| 14 | Virginia at 90 | 135 |

# Terminology

Virginia Prince's full birth name was Arnold Lowman (no middle name) and when describing him in his younger days we shall use this name. As an adult, Virginia elected to use the name Charles Prince as a masculine pseudonym and therefore this will be used when appropriate. The use of he or she and him or her will be used in whichever way seems to offer the greatest clarity. For many years the former Arnold Lowman has chosen to be known as Virginia Prince within the transgender community; however, her legal name is Virginia Bruce.

The terms transvestism and cross dressing will be considered synonymous. As used here, the terms transgenderism and transsexualism both designate a person living entirely in the gender role opposite his or her biological sex. We will use Virginia's term, *transgenderist,* when no gender reassignment surgery has been undertaken.

# Photo credits

The Lowman and Prince pictures were provided by Virginia Prince from family albums and *Transvestia* magazine. Mariette Pathy Allen, a renowned photographer, took the picture on page vii. The typography and cover graphics were assembled by Richard Docter with the help of Shirley Docter. Cover photo by Patti Thomas.

# Chronology

| YEAR | AGE | EVENT |
|------|-----|-------|
| 1912 | Birth | Born in Los Angeles, November 23, 1912 |
| 1916 | 4 | Birth of sister |
| 1921 | 9 | Residential elementary school, grades 3 - 7 |
| 1924 | 12 | Began fetishistic cross dressing |
| 1926 | 14 | Complete cross dressing; nighttime neighborhood walks |
| 1928 | 16 | Bus trips as Muriel to downtown Los Angeles |
| 1930 | 18 | Graduation from Los Angeles High School |
| 1931 | 19 | Enrolled in Pomona College |
| 1935 | 23 | B.A., Pomona College with Honors in Chemistry |

| | | |
|---|---|---|
| 1937 | 25 | M.A., University of California, Berkeley, in Pharmacology |
| 1939 | 27 | Ph.D., University of California, Berkeley, in Pharmacology |
| 1941 | 29 | Married to Dorothy Shepherd |
| 1941-1942 | 29 | Graduate Research Assistant, UC Medical School, San Francisco. Assumed name of Virginia Prince. |
| 1942-1947 | 29-35 | Research Biochemist |
| 1946 | 34 | Birth of son, Brent |
| 1948-1968 | 36-55 | Co-owner, Cardinal Industries |
| 1951 | 38 | Divorced from Dorothy Shepherd |
| 1953 | 40 | Superior court suit over child visitation rights and alimony |
| 1955 | 42 | Began taking female hormones (for about six years) |

| 1956 | 44 | Married Doreen Skinner |
| 1960 | 48 | Founded Transvestia Magazine |
| 1961 | 49 | Federal prosecution for mailing "obscene material" |
| 1962 | 50 | Met Dr. Robert Stoller, UCLA psychiatrist |
| 1962 | 50 | Commenced lectures for service clubs and colleges |
| 1962 | 50 | Probation terminated |
| 1966 | 54 | Divorced Doreen Skinner |
| 1968 | 55 | Began living full-time as a woman, June, 1968 |
| 1968 | 55 | Sold ownership in Cardinal Industries |
| 1976 | 63 | Son Brent died |
| 1980 | 68 | Concluded editorship of Transvestia Magazine |
| 1986 | 74 | Recipient of Lifetime Achievement Award from International Foundation for Gender Education |

| 1991 | 79 | Psychiatrist and friend, Dr. Robert Stoller died |
| 1997 | 85 | Honored at California State University, Northridge, 85th birthday party |
| 2000 | 88 | Sold home, moved to Claremont retirement community |

# CHAPTER 1

# Introduction

## *The Good Samaritan*

Just before noon, on Saturday, November 23, 2002, I was sitting in the living room at the home of Virginia Prince in Claremont, California. Two of my California State University, Northridge colleagues, historian Vern Bullough and psychologist Richard Smith, both retired professors just as I am, had joined me in visiting Virginia to wish her a happy 90th birthday. I noticed a small bible with an old, worn, leather binding at the end of her bookshelf and opened it to discover the baptismal record of Arnold Lowman, Virginia's given name. This religious ceremony had occurred exactly 89 years earlier to the day, on his first birthday. The baptism was conducted by the pastor of the prestigious and imposing First Congregational Church of Los Angeles where the Lowman family were active members.

Examining that page in the bible, I tried to imagine the feelings of the Lowmans that day, and what their expectations might have been for their first-born son. Would he strive to emulate his physician father or would he walk in the footsteps of his more commercially motivated and somewhat mannish mother? Whatever hopes and dreams they might have shared standing before their pastor, they almost certainly never could have anticipated Virginia's remarkable career as an internationally recognized organizer of transgendered persons. Certainly, Virginia's college educated and religious parents could not have envisioned that their infant son, by the age of 55, would surrender both her baptismal name and her masculine identity and live the rest of her life as a woman.

Arnold Lowman (Virginia Prince) was born on November 23, 1912 at the *Good Samaritan Hospital* in downtown Los Angeles following what is believed to have been an uneventful full-term pregnancy and birth. This was Mrs. Lowman's first child. How ironic that this venerable hospital would be named for the Good Samaritan who cared so deeply for the social outcast, the victim, the person shunned by respectable travelers on that dusty road so long ago. In many ways, Virginia Prince seems to have emulated the life and values of the first Good Samaritan.

The initial chapters of this book tell the story of a young man who became a typical fetishistic cross dresser, married and became a father, then divorced to remarry nine years later. During these years his cross dressing skills were perfected, a process we describe in detail because in many ways it serves as a trail guide to the decades of practice often seen across the lifespan of the cross dresser. Over many years, Prince gradually developed a small circle of transvestite friends. We describe how important it was to Virginia to affiliate with these other cross dressers, and how this led to her taking leadership in organizing local and national support groups. Virginia then founded Transvestia magazine and edited it for twenty years, all the time striving to help establish new transgender support groups both in the United States and overseas. Without question, Prince became the most influential leader in the formative years of the transgender rights movement.

Beginning in 1962, Prince met regularly for twenty-nine years with Dr. Robert Stoller, a UCLA psychiatrist who recorded their discussions about sex and gender. These materials are confidential research records, acquired under conditions of confidentiality that assured the anonymity of Prince, a procedure scrupulously followed by Stoller. Virginia has not read these typewritten materials and has never listened to the tape recordings. She does not recall much of the interview content that had been discussed. I have not hesitated to select passages from these transcripts that tell us of her fantasies, her conflicts, and her sexual behavior and I have asked Virginia to review my comments because the material originated in a confidential research setting, and she has done so without requesting any changes. A word about the references to these transcripts: I have numbered the transcribed interviews sequentially by date, from 1 to 33, each representing a set of double-spaced typewritten material of roughly twenty or thirty pages in length. My reference will give the number of the set (e.g., Stoller, #1...) followed by the page number within that set. Stoller was killed in an automobile accident in September, 1991 near his residence, and his wife later directed that both the tape recordings and the transcripts be given to Virginia Prince. These interviews provide a remarkable inventory of information about Virginia's transgender and sexual history.

In the final part of this book we describe one of Prince's main ideas about transgender behavior -- the concept of the "girl within." This concept connected transgender feelings to the sense of selfhood long before many others

7

adopted this view. Finally, we give the history of some serious difficulties that were very punishing to Prince: First, the breakup of the original Chapter and finally, her prosecution on a charge of mailing so-called obscene material. We shall turn now to the story of the family of Virginia Prince

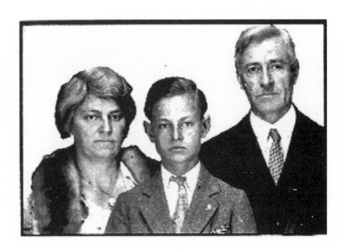

*Dr. and Mrs. Lowman and their son, Arnold*

## CHAPTER 2

# The Family

## *Charles LeRoy Lowman, M.D.*

Virginia's father was born in Park Ridge, Illinois, a suburb of Chicago, in 1879. According to a newspaper article published after his death, Lowman had arrived in Los Angeles by train at the age of 21 with ten dollars in his wallet. He soon found a job as a bill collector for an ice company. Lowman had worked briefly for the forest service and as a State Highway Commission employee before attending the University of Southern California Medical School, not far from the Adams Boulevard area where he later would establish the Orthopedic Hospital. Lowman completed his medical training in Boston and soon returned to become one of the first orthopedic surgeons in southern California. He became a highly regarded physician in Los Angeles and worked closely with school board leaders to assist school children with special needs. After decades of service an elementary school was named in his honor.

Dr. Lowman was strongly entrepreneurial but not in the commercial sense of this term. He was far more inclined to be a caring, giving, and altruistic physician. In 1909 he enlisted some volunteers from a nearby bible school to help him form a Crippled Children's Guild that provided medical assistance to low income families. His landlord at the time was a wealthy real estate developer, John Brockman, who knew of Lowman's desire to open a hospital dedicated to serving needful children. Brockman purchased what remained of an extensive Los Angeles estate following a fire that destroyed one of the opulent Adams District mansions. All that remained was a large, elaborate stable, a fishpond, and a gazebo, and Brockman offered it to Lowman as a gift providing he could raise $100,000 to establish a hospital within three years. This was accomplished. The stable was remodeled and became the first structure of Dr. Lowman's new hospital.

During World War, I Lowman served as an Army doctor stationed in San Francisco at Letterman Army Hospital. Later, he maintained a private practice in the Pacific Mutual building in downtown Los Angeles while directing the Orthopedic Hospital. The Lowmans were a financially comfortable family but according to Virginia "…we were never part of the Beverly Hills crowd, and we didn't think of ourselves as rich." While they were not among the wealthy country club set, they were financially and socially far above the status of most of the citizens of Los Angeles.

During Arnold's first eight years, the Lowmans lived at 123 South Hobart Street. This was a very attractive upper middle-class neighborhood of single family homes located just south of Beverly Boulevard and three blocks east of Western Avenue, a part of the great westward expansion of the city. Like most of Los Angeles, these former farm lands were laid out along section lines with a grid of east-west streets. The spacious homes along Hobart Street have remained largely unchanged over the past 90 years.

Like many physicians, Dr. Lowman's work required many hours away from the family. He was noted both for the origination of innovative therapies for the youthful victims of polio, and also for an open door policy that admitted virtually every child in need regardless of their ability to pay. Virginia commented: "In some ways, the hospital was sort of my father's family and we came in second." Reflecting on some family relationships at the age of 87, Virginia said "I think my father may have favored my sister somewhat, but I always admired him greatly."

As an early southern California surgeon, Dr. Charles LeRoy Lowman was later honored in many ways for his contributions to his community. Dr. Lowman's 90th birthday party was held at the Palladium, a forties era dance pavilion on Sunset Boulevard, attended by over 1500 of his former patients and their families, and hosted by Art Linkletter. The love of his life, the Orthopedic Hospital, is now a part of the UCLA Medical School network of hospitals. Dr. Lowman died in Los Angeles at the age of 98. Virginia described him as "…a

11

pioneer orthopedic surgeon especially concerned with the treatment of polio…and he was a lot more interested in helping poor kids than he was in being a society doctor." He was "…not a hail fellow, well met sort of man…rather, he was more aloof than that."

Many years later, when describing Dr. Lowman to psychiatrist Robert Stoller, she remembered her father somewhat less generously than in the years following his death. She portrayed him as a "complex" person who cared little for making money, a father who could not find the time to attend the high school track meets of his only son, and a husband, who in his later years, grew sufficiently distant from his wife that they moved into separate bedrooms. She explained to Stoller: "My dad was a complex character…he not only never made much money, he never aspired to do so. Dad was altruistic. My mother made most of the money in the family, from real estate and stocks" (Stoller, #24, p. 14-15).

During his son's elementary school years, Dr. Lowman came to believe Arnold was not as tall as he should have been and he consulted with a long-time friend and Orthopedic Hospital colleague who was an endocrinologist. Together, they decided that Arnold should try taking some growth hormones. These may or may not have had an impact upon Virginia's ultimate height, which Virginia said was about five feet, eight inches. In 2003, her actual measurement was five feet, five inches. Looking back, a more important question would be whether Arnold's physician father perceived him as not only shorter than expected, but also less strong or even less masculine than hoped for. Virginia believes this was not the case. "Yes, he wanted me to grow taller, but he certainly never considered me a pantywaist." Today, Virginia consistently plays down even the most moderate criticism of her parents, although she expressed some strong feelings of resentment toward her father in the Stoller interviews. Age has a way of helping us to forgive and to forget. One good example of this came out when she met with Dr. Stoller in 1985. She first told him that "I have a feeling that I somehow gave you a more negative feeling about my relationship (with my father) than is valid" (Stoller, #31, p. 14). She then offered Stoller several examples of Dr. Lowman giving attention, such as attending college track meets when Arnold was running cross country races. Stoller, however, was persistent in asking about how demonstrative Dr. Lowman was toward Arnold. Virginia explained: "Well, it's true, he wasn't demonstrative the way I've seen other fathers (as when) introducing their son to somebody else, like, 'This is my boy Charlie'…and he wasn't demonstrative with me the way he was with my sister…he would hold her, kiss her and hug her, which he wasn't doing to me" (p. 15). "I must have had some sense of deprivation or annoyance or hurt or resentment or something like that, or this would not have made such an impression on me while he was still alive" (p. 15). These hurts and resentments would echo throughout his life.

Arnold's cross dressing also contributed significantly to a stressful relationship with his father. For example, much later, in 1953, two years after his divorce from his first wife, Arnold went to court seeking modification of his visiting rights and reduction of alimony payments. This trial produced colorful newspaper accounts about Arnold Lowman, the transvestite, along with photographs of him and his former wife. At the Lowman's home the response to this publicity was extremely negative, and Arnold was threatened with being disowned. At this time something quite surprising occurred.

13

According to Virginia's report to Stoller, the Lowman's live-in housekeeper, Doreen, who would later marry Arnold, saw "...some pictures of my dad in dresses, and heard him making some kind of comment to her (such as)...he's just like me" (Stoller, #24, p. 17). Virginia then added: "If he had an inferiority complex because of his own transvestic interests, that could have washed over back onto me. It might have made him more sensitive to my lack of being a football fullback, or my (lack of) manliness" (p. 18). Today, Virginia insists that even if his father "did put on a dress" it did not have anything to do with the father and son relationship. We cannot assess the accuracy of this assertion, but we can say with certainty that when Virginia "came out" to her father, he showed no empathy, understanding, or acceptance of her transvestism. He remained very rejecting toward Virginia for the rest of his life. As a result, Virginia had a very disappointing life-long relationship with her father, respecting him highly for his professional achievements, yet longing for a more intimate sense of support and caring. This remains one of the major disappointments and unfilled needs in her life. The love and appreciation Arnold longed for was provided, at least in part, by his mother, although she may not have made Arnold one of her top priorities. Mrs. Lowman, as we shall see, was very much the business woman.

Virginia has recounted to me what must have been one of the most painful episodes in her life. This dealt with her first effort to explain her transvestism to her father. She was obviously seeking his understanding and approval and she was also confessing to him this long-held secret life. Still in her twenties and just prior to World War II, Arnold had been on a trip to San Francisco, having spent the entire weekend as Virginia. Upon returning, he telephoned his father, asking him to meet near Exposition Park. He arrived as agreed, and Virginia walked to his car, entered the car, and explained that "...this is the real person who I am...my father was shocked ..." Dr. Lowman's grasp of transvestism was not only quite limited, but his proposed plan of action was considerably misdirected. He concluded that his son was deficient in male hormones and urged supplemental testosterone. Virginia declined.

Virginia tried several different ways to open the door to a more rewarding relationship with her father. Chatting over lunch with a cheerful smile, she has told me more than once a story of the kindness and understanding shown by the secretary of her father concerning Virginia's cross dressing. After Virginia had confided in this woman about her cross dressing, she invited Virginia to her home. "One time," Virginia recounts, "after this lady showed real understanding of my needs, I went to her and asked that she purchase a black teddy that my father could then give me as a gift." Virginia describes this as an effort to allow her father to show acceptance of her cross dressing. The secretary bought this lingerie, wrapped it as a gift, and arranged for Dr. Lowman to present it as a birthday present. He did so, but without any evidence that he had become more understanding of Virginia's feminine side. "I still have it...," Virginia said, proudly treasuring this special keepsake from her father. This was not the first or the last time that Virginia would manipulate some kind of reward though the kindness of a woman who would befriend her.

As seen by Virginia, her father never came to appreciate her many international efforts to stimulate a movement in support of transgendered people, her founding of Transvestia magazine, or her achievement of a doctorate from the University of California. How unfortunate that this doctor's son could earn international celebrity as a helping, constructive, hard-working organizer and leader, yet fail to garner the respect of his father. "He never really came to accept me as Virginia," she said. In later years, following Arnold's second divorce, "I attempted to make peace and invited them to have dinner with me, and they did so, but only once." Prince faithfully visited his mother during her final years in an assisted care facility near downtown Los Angeles, but he seldom saw or even spoke with his father by telephone.

We should keep in mind that around 1940, when Virginia first presented herself to her father, both the civil rights movement and the drive for decriminalization of homosexuality and transgender behavior remained at least a quarter of a century away. Dr. Lowman had grown up during the late nineteenth century and he very likely held social, sexual, and gender attitudes that were common among his socioeconomic and ethnic peers at that time. Virginia sighed when she summarized her father's social views: "He was just the product of his times...he never really understood much about homosexuality or cross dressing..." At times Virginia portrays her father as a charming and likeable family leader, and at other times as "rejecting" and distant. Without doubt, Dr. Lowman considered homosexuality as immoral sexual misconduct, and he seems to have perceived a clear link between this widely regarded "improper" behavior and cross dressing. Throughout the life of Virginia Prince we shall see many examples of how this homophobic perspective affected Dr. Lowman, his son, and their relationship.

Later we shall describe the many interviews between Virginia Prince and psychiatrist Robert Stoller. Based on what

Prince told him, Stoller developed a view of the father and son relationship much like I have described. He dictated this note to himself that helps to complete our impression of a very disappointing father-son relationship:

*"Famous father, who Prince invariably felt was disappointed in him and never admired him, never praised him, never paid attention to him except to express dissatisfaction. And his father, in order to create a successful career, was rarely home. Prince's mother who was more with him was even more powerful than his father, for she was not only a great mover of social organizations, but she visibly loved and clearly dominated her husband"* (Stoller, #8, p. 14).

If Stoller is right about Mrs. Lowman's power, we are left with the question of why she did not insist upon a more even-handed father and son relationship.

During the final years of Dr. Lowman's life, he married for a second time; this wife was not sympathetic toward Prince. Virginia made one of her rare appearances dressed in masculine attire to call upon her famous father at his home in the Hollywood hills. He was not invited inside. Apparently, the doctor who could offer help to everybody else's child could not forgive the disappointments he felt about his son. Charles LeRoy Lowman died at the age of 98, adored and honored by hundreds of his former patients. He was a great doctor and medical leader; his skills as a father were very limited. Prince dug deeply into his closet for one of Charles' suits and attended Dr. Lowman's funeral without taking an active role.

17

# Elizabeth Hudson (Arnold) Lowman

Virginia's mother, Elizabeth Hudson Arnold, was born into a prominent professional family in Galesburg, Indiana, the daughter of Benjamin Franklin Arnold and Ella Ferris. The family owned a farm and also invested in real estate. Compared to most of their neighbors, they were well off.

The Ferris family took pride in recalling that Virginia's great-great grandfather was George Washington Ferris, the inventor of the spectacular Ferris wheel that first appeared at the 1893 Chicago Exposition, rising 266 feet above the fairgrounds. Virginia's mother was primarily dedicated to raising her two children, running a busy household, and serving as the wife of a socially important physician who needed to reach out to raise money to support his Orthopedic Hospital which grew steadily both in size and importance. She also made a significant contribution to the income of the family by investing in real estate and by developing both housing and industrial properties.

Mrs. Lowman is described in less than one sentence in Volume 100 of Transvestia as "...a mother who was a very capable woman in real estate, investments and other, at the time, rather un-feminine ways" (p. 5). With Stoller, Virginia occasionally described her as somewhat "mannish." Could that description apply to more than her business pursuits in real estate? One may also wonder about the possible significance of such a brief and unrevealing account of her own mother, especially since whatever parent-child affection was shown to Arnold came from Mrs. Lowman. But this brevity might be explained by Virginia's ambivalent feelings about letting others know much about the Lowman family. She was of two minds on this topic. For the most part, she maintained a strict boundary separating all of the life of Virginia Prince from the lives of her family. Until recently, the identity of her physician father was seldom discussed, even with good friends. On the other hand, she consistently found ways to share this information with a few professionals, clearly feeling pride in the achievements of the Lowmans.

From a financial standpoint, the Lowman family continued to thrive during Arnold's childhood. After moving from 123 South Hobart Avenue when Arnold was eight, the Lowmans settled into an upscale district two blocks off Wilshire Boulevard, at 867 Victoria Avenue in the exclusive Hancock Park neighborhood. It was here that in later years many celebrities would own homes, including Nat King Cole and J. Paul Getty. The Victoria Avenue home was about three blocks from the intersection of Wilshire and Crenshaw Boulevards, where the cross dressed Virginia would soon be taking buses into downtown Los Angeles. Hancock Park remains one of the most elegant and expensive neighborhoods in West Los Angeles.

Taken as a whole, the family life of the Lowmans throughout these growing-up years is remembered by Virginia as "nothing out of the ordinary." Both parents were very hard working examples of the Protestant ethic. But while both Dr. Lowman and Arnold's mother were busy people, today Virginia reports she has little sense of feeling deprived of parental attention or approval. She puts it this way: "People sometimes try to look back on their childhood and blame their parents for something that didn't work out well in their life, but that's not true of my childhood. Yes, my father was very busy as a doctor and with starting the hospital, but he spent a good deal of time with his family." This idealized view is totally in contrast with the far less complimentary perception of family relationships described to Robert Stoller; we'll say more about this later.

If Virginia Prince needed role models for entrepreneurial initiative, reasonable risk-taking, and organizational skills, each of her parents seemed to fill this role very nicely. Both parents were strongly dedicated as entrepreneurs; they did not seek to become wealthy, but earning a little extra money was not seen as a bad thing. Both seemed to be good financial managers. They were both especially committed to the development of the Orthopedic Hospital as a service for the less fortunate. Each parent was highly motivated for achievement in his and her own way and we may assume that some of this rubbed off on their son. Judging from his school performance from the elementary years through earning a Ph.D. in Pharmacology, Arnold tended to follow the rules, keep his eye on the prize, and achieve one academic goal after the other. He was never, however, the most outstanding of students, and he viewed himself as both physically undersized compared to his peers, and socially inadequate. Arnold did not date until his senior year in high school.

In the 1940's when Virginia was about 30 and her cross dressing was of growing importance in her life, she made several attempts to gain the support and understanding of her father. These efforts were not successful. At the time, according to Virginia's recollection, Dr. Lowman asked that she not reveal this to Mrs. Lowman, and Prince did not do so. Some years later, upon being informed of Virginia's transvestism, Mrs. Lowman was surprised but far more supportive than her husband had been. She soon entered into an arrangement with her son, allowing him to borrow some of her clothing provided he did not damage them, an offer Virginia seldom accepted. Mrs. Lowman lived to be 86.

## Elizabeth Lowman

The second and final Lowman child was a daughter, Elizabeth, born four years after Arnold. While Arnold "borrowed her clothes a few times" the two did not seem close. From Virginia's comments, she was very envious of her younger sister who always seemed to gather the attention and affection of her father, while young Arnold looked on, wondering what it would take to receive the warmth of Dr. Lowman's affection. While Virginia has commented on these feeling of envy, today she cautions that we should not make too much of this. Today, Virginia looks upon both her parents and her sister through rose-colored glasses.

There is substantial evidence that envy of Elizabeth played an important part in Arnold's growing up years. For example, twenty years ago, in Prince's many interviews with Dr. Stoller, Virginia told him: "She was a very attractive girl. She was popular when she got into high school, good looking, and I was envious of her" (Stoller, #24, p. 9).

We may certainly wonder if this theme of envy, or perhaps identification, might have played a part in Arnold's initial fetishistic cross dressing, and his striving to appear to be an attractive woman. He discussed this in 1983: "My desire to dress in girls' clothing and to be the girl in the mirror was to acquire some of the same social graces, the social appeal, and the social ease (of girls)" ( Stoller, #24, p. 6).

21

Elizabeth was very popular in high school and young men were calling upon her at the Prince home quite frequently. Following high school she enrolled at Pomona college and joined the Delta Delta Delta sorority, greatly pleasing her mother. She only remained there for a year, then transferred to the University of California, Berkeley. Prince is unsure of what her major was. There she met and later married a mining engineer and moved to Nevada where he was employed as a mine superintendent. She has lived in Nevada all of her adult life.

Until the age of 55 and the emergence of a full-time Virginia Prince, Arnold would occasionally travel to the Las Vegas area to visit his sister, but these trips became less frequent following Arnold's transgender transition. There seems never to have been a close relationship between them, and following their last meeting when Virginia was 89 she told me "…we just don't think the same way about a lot of things." She wondered if that would be their final visit. For several years, Elizabeth has been living in a retirement community. Prince's relationship with Elizabeth, his only close relative, seems to be a template for the many disappointing relationships she has had throughout her life. First, there was the very disappointing relationship with her father and to a lesser extent, with her mother, accompanied by the failure of two marriages and the death of her son, and finally the feeling that her sister had little in common with her. In all, we must ask: Who did Virginia really love throughout her life, and who really loved her.

# CHAPTER 3

# Education

## *Elementary to High School*

Virginia's family did not aspire to belong to the elite group of wealthy physicians in Los Angeles – "the Beverly Hills crowd" as Virginia put it, but for the Lowmans there was never any financial pressure, even during the depression years of the 1930's. When it came time for school, Virginia began in the public schools but was transferred to a private residential school -- the Glendora Foothill School, for grades three through seven. Glendora is about fifty miles east of downtown Los Angeles, and at the time it could be reached by use of the Pacific Electric Railway system. Most of the time Arnold would return home on the Big Red Cars "every two or three weeks," and at other times the parents would visit him "for a horse show, or some special event at the school." The reasons for sending Arnold to a residential school are not clear, but my guess is that perhaps the parents thought some deficiency in Arnold's academic progress could be overcome by placing him in a residential facility. We know of nothing unusual about Lowman's academic or personal development during these years. Apparently, the wife of the Headmaster at this school was an attractive, supportive, and caring person who has been remembered fondly by Virginia. She recalls having "quite a crush on her."

On Thanksgiving Day, when Arnold had just begun the seventh grade, the school burned down and he was immediately enrolled in John Burroughs Junior High School. This school was close to his home on the west side of the city, an upper middle class and totally white school at that time, as were most of the Los Angeles public schools. Arnold went on to attend Los Angeles High School, graduating in the class of 1931. His favorite courses were in the sciences, especially Chemistry. His favorite athletic activity was running on the cross country track team. Talking with Stoller, he minimizes the importance of this noting that because of his size he was a member of the "Class C" team, not the varsity. Judging from the comments students jotted down in a high school yearbook, the teen-age Arnold was well recognized for his work in chemistry, algebra and various laboratory courses. One of the more prescient comments from a buddy was this: "Good Luck, You'll need it" (Anonymous, Los Angeles High School Yearbook, Winter, 1930). None of these high school classmates became life-long friends. From everything I have learned about Arnold's performance in school during these years, he seemed to be a strong student academically, definitely less "forward" in dating than most of the men, and while he had many friends, he was not one of the most outstanding members of his class.

## Pomona College

At the age of 19, and with understandable anxiety, Arnold enrolled for the Fall semester of 1931 in Pomona College, one of the most prestigious small, residential liberal arts colleges in southern California. While riding with me on a drive through the campus in 2001, she delighted in showing off the elegant tree-lined college. With ample ivy growing on some of the older buildings and beautiful lawns and stately eucalyptus trees, Pomona has long been one of California's premier small private colleges. Virginia now lives within walking distance of her old dorm room. Here, as chemistry major, Arnold seemed to grow increasingly confident and successful, never suspecting that one of the other men in the dorm would begin living as a woman within a decade -- more than 20 years before his own gender transition into Virginia. This former classmate was the first of two transgendered persons presented at case conferences at the medical school while Virginia was working as a post-doctoral research assistant at the University of California Medical Center in San Francisco. We'll describe more about this later.

*Arnold (upper left) and his cross country track team*

At Pomona College, in addition to his academic work, Virginia was Co-Captain of the cross country track team and participated in intercollegiate track meets. In a four mile race around the Rose Bowl she broke her fibula at the half-way mark, but managed to finish. Academically, he continued to be most interested in the sciences and he maintained above average grades while not reaching the top of his class. "In college," Virginia mused, "I always thought of myself as a B student."

## Graduate School

Arnold Lowman graduated with a B.A. degree in Chemistry from Pomona College in June, 1935 and was immediately accepted as a graduate student at the University of California. Much of his graduate work was in San Francisco, a city he had come to know and enjoy very much. His area of specialization was in pharmacology, but that is not the same as a school for the training of pharmacists. Arnold specialized in the development of medication and in pharmacological research. He earned a master's degree in 1937, and then went on to a doctoral program with the same specialization. The Doctor of Philosophy degree was awarded to him in Pharmacology, in 1939. Arnold moved back to Los Angeles for about two years and worked for several companies, including Baxter Laboratories, Horton-Converse, and Anabolic Foods.

His life took several new turns during a single weekend in 1941, when he was married to Dorothy Shepherd, then drove to Santa Barbara for a short honeymoon, and then on to a new job with Del Monte Foods in Oakland, California. Soon the newlyweds moved to Berkeley where they lived for two years. One of his University professors had received funding for a research project and he recruited his former student to assist him at the University's medical school campus near Golden Gate Park in San Francisco. For six months, Arnold left their

Berkeley apartment, took a ferryboat to the foot of Market Street, and finally rode a streetcar to his new job

It was during this period that he was to learn about Louise Lawrence, an influential cross dresser, and arrange to meet her. Although Arnold was not working in the Department of Psychiatry, he gave special attention to their clinical training seminars. He noted two case presentations involving transgendered males and attended both. The first case to be presented turned out to be his former Pomona classmate who was by this time living full-time as a woman: Edward "Tug" Richards had become Barbara Ann Wilcox and she was among the earliest sexually reassigned males in America, predating Christine Jorgensen by about a decade. Later, her wife was also sexually reassigned However, beyond Arnold's being very surprised by this development, he had no further connection with Wilcox. Prince say's that Wilcox had "...faked a urine test by substituting her wife's sample..." thereby passing herself off to physicians as an Intersex person to gain her surgery.

The second case was that of Louise Lawrence and Arnold made it his business to discover her address and contact her at home. We shall explain the Lawrence relationship more fully in Chapter 5

*Arnold Lowman*

## CHAPTER 4

# Two Marriages

## *Dorothy Shepherd*

Arnold met Dorothy S. Shepherd at their church and they fell in love. She was a year older than Arnold. We know almost nothing of her early life or of her family; both her mother and a sister lived in Los Angeles. At least some of the time she worked as a secretary. In 1941, Arnold and Dorothy were married in Los Angeles at the home of his parents, and, as we've noted, they immediately moved to the bay area for a new job he had accepted.

Virginia had not revealed his cross dressing to Dorothy prior to the marriage. Promising himself to give up all cross dressing after marrying, Arnold burned all of his carefully-acquired women's clothing the night before the wedding. He was certain that this was the end of his career as a cross dresser. "I didn't cross dress a single time for the first three months," she told me, "then when my wife was away for a Thanksgiving weekend it all came surging back." Arnold had been somewhat careless in how some of his wife's clothing had been returned to the dresser drawers, and when confronted about this "...well, I just mumbled something about...I didn't know what had disturbed the clothing." Dorothy never became comfortable with Virginia's cross dressing and this appears to have been a major factor in their divorce. Their first extensive discussion about cross dressing did not occur until the second year of their marriage. At the conclusion of Prince's one year research assignment at the University medical center, they returned to southern California, living in a house in west Los Angeles. He went to work as a chemist.

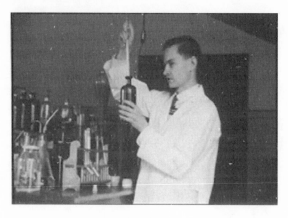

*At 27, Arnold Lowman earned a Ph.D. in Pharmacology*

Their only child, a son, Brent, was born on the first of July, 1946 at the same hospital where Arnold Lowman had been born -- the Good Samaritan. During their seven year marriage most of Virginia's cross dressing episodes were done both secretly and apart from Dorothy. These outings typically involved trips to window-shop, eating in cafeterias and restaurants, and cautiously engaging in other low-risk public adventures. Dorothy had become progressively less happy in the marriage, a fact her husband was slow to recognize. During 1951, while visiting family members in the Midwest, Dorothy consulted a psychiatrist and sought his guidance. As described by Prince, he advised her that, in his view, "transvestism involved homosexuality," and he urged her to obtain a divorce. Upon returning to Los Angeles, without warning, she telephoned Virginia at work and reported that she had left him for good, that she had taken both their young son and the family silver, and that she had moved in with her sister in Hollywood. They were divorced in 1951. Recounting this break-up over lunch with me in a Hollywood coffee shop a few years ago, Virginia presented it in a logical, step-by-step chronology but with little feeling or emotion. Perhaps the years that have passed have lessened the painful experience that separation must have been. At the time, Prince went to the sister-in-law's apartment, pounded on the locked door and could hear his son crying. The police were called but no action was taken as nothing improper had been done. The break-up was an enormous loss to Prince, possibly tapping into his feelings of lack of parental approval and his fragile self-esteem. The minimizing of the significance of this divorce is part of a well-established defense whereby the losses and intense interpersonal hurts of the past are intellectualized as nothing more than the give and take of everyday life, an emotionally protective tactic that is very much a part of Prince.

31

*Arnold Lowman at 37 with his son, Brent*

Dorothy maintained strict control over the visitation rights of her former husband and was not as cooperative as she might have been. In early March, 1953 Arnold, then 40, initiated a suit asking the Superior Court to award him more visitation time with his son and to reduce his alimony payments. Dorothy hired what Virginia recalls as "a nasty lawyer" who was eager to have Arnold's cross dressing activities brought out as evidence of his unsuitability as a father. Throughout the four day trial there was extensive courtroom use of the words "transvestism" and "masturbation," according to Prince.

At least four Los Angeles newspapers covered this trial with explicit descriptions of Virginia's "transvestite" behavior. One headline read: "Man Who Dons Women's Attire Wins Son Case." Another paper headlined their extensive coverage: "Admits He Is A Transvestite -- Tells Court He Likes to Dress as Woman." The judge ruled in favor of Arnold. He was to have the right to visit Brent "at any reasonable time" and to take him with him one day a week, from 10 a. m. until 9 p. m. While Dorothy, then age 41, won an increase in child support payments from $50 to $60 per month, her alimony payments of $50 monthly were ordered to be discontinued as she had obtained employment as a secretary.

*Virginia was 38 in 1951 and between marriages*

It was shown during the trial that Virginia had developed credible skills in presenting herself as a woman. When called to testify, Dorothy's mother, Mrs. Clara Shepherd, went to the witness stand presumably to give evidence that Virginia had indeed been out in public dressed as a woman, something he had already admitted. She told the court that on a particular Sunday, following a church service, she had been "accosted on the street as she left the church" by a "very well-dressed and refined lady" who turned out to be her son-in-law, who was also emerging from church. Apparently, painting Arnold as a transvestite had no impact upon the court.

Prince's son, Brent went on to marry, and to have a son of his own, but Virginia has never had a relationship with this grandchild and doesn't know where he lives. Brent had a troubled life and he died in 1976, very possibly a suicide. He was 30. The facts surrounding this tragedy are not clear and Virginia is not at ease discussing it.

During the first marriage, despite Arnold's Ph.D. in pharmacology, he only worked for a year or two in this rapidly expanding and high paying industry. For the most part, Arnold stuck to his first interest which was chemistry. Into his 30s, he worked as a chemist, analyzing products and helping to develop lotions and other beauty and pet products. An early product was a novel way to remove nail polish through immersion of the nail tip in a gelatin-like substance. Another product was designed to help prevent runs in the new nylon stockings that became favored following World War II. Greater commercial success was found for the many lotions, shampoos and skin products that were created. The customers were typically beauty salons and veterinary clinics.

*Courtroom photographs of Arnold and Dorothy, 1953*

A fellow worker brought a product proposal to Arnold for the development of a hair straightening shampoo to be sold to "colored people." They developed this, marketed it successfully in a modest way, and went on to bring other

34

beauty and veterinary and chemical products to the retail market. With a partner, Prince established Cardinal Industries. The facilities for manufacturing these goods were on real estate developed and owned by his mother, near Pico and Highland in West Los Angeles. The business prospered and is still operating, although it later was bought by a larger company. Arnold sold his interest to his partner in 1968, netting about a 1000% gain from his initial investment. He also profited following the sale of the building.

## Doreen Skinner

About five years after divorcing Dorothy, Virginia married again. The second wife, Doreen Skinner, born and raised in England, had served as a live-in housekeeper for the Lowman family and she had extensive knowledge of Virginia's ever-growing interest in cross dressing; initially, she was not comfortable with this. However, upon coming to know Arnold as a dating partner, she learned more about the meaning of this to Arnold and she then showed far greater acceptance. Doreen had made a very positive impression upon Mrs. Lowman while working in their home, and it was Mrs. Lowman who became the matchmaker. Years later, Prince said, "…we were more or less thrown together by my mother, and that's how we came to be married." In many ways, it proved to be one of the most intense and most fulfilling relationships Prince was ever to enjoy, despite the breakup ten years later.

When they first began dating, Arnold found Doreen to be unattractive because of her "dowdy attire, old fashioned hair style and lack of makeup." Virginia told me, "I took her down to the beach and explained in simple English what she needed to do to spruce her self up and become a more attractive

35

woman." Doreen took this advice and with Arnold's assistance, she bought some new clothing and did a major makeover with her appearance. Soon they were dating on a regular basis, and Virginia began to tell her more about his ever-growing interest in cross dressing. She became far more supportive of this, and soon thereafter she encouraged Virginia to dress when she visited his apartment. Following their marriage, they would meet and go out socially as two women, and occasionally they went to San Francisco with Virginia living as a woman for several days.

*Doreen and Virginia*

As a wedding gift, the new Mrs. Arnold Lowman presented Virginia with "...a lovely white satin nightgown." Following their marriage, they acquired a lot in the Hollywood Hills and designed a house with a view. All went well "...for about seven years," but this marriage also ended in divorce despite what seemed to have been extensive participation by Doreen in Virginia's business activities, and also in Virginia's fantasy sex life. Virginia revealed to Robert Stoller (see the Introduction concerning these transcripts) that some of his most gratifying sexual experiences were with Doreen, especially when she would pretend to be a man, having sex with Virginia as the woman. Prince told Stoller that she believed the "epitome of joy" for the transvestite was having sex with a woman while cross dressed. This was a frequent delight during his marriage to Doreen. While she was not outwardly a person with much of an interest in sex, on rare occasions she surprised Prince with her erotic boldness and initiative, both of which were much appreciated.

Historian Vern Bullough and his wife Bonnie were invited to have dinner at the home of the Princes in about 1964; they had come to know them as friends. Bonnie later noted that with Virginia acting as the hostess for their meal together "...there didn't seem to be a role for a wife." Many years later, Vern Bullough speculated that "Virginia may have been so concerned about her own feminine role and having her own needs fulfilled by others, that there was little investment in meeting the needs of Doreen." He remembered Doreen as a somewhat plain, even dowdy lady, and a soft-spoken woman "...who in some ways slipped into the role of the maid for Virginia...like the chief cook and bottle washer." Years before, Prince had taken them on a tour of the house he and Doreen had designed and built in Nichols Canyon. This included a special closet that was the entrance to a room set aside for Virginia, complete with her wardrobe closets, a sewing machine and several mirrors. Bullough regards himself as a good, long-time friend of Virginia's, and they have collaborated on several research projects. When I had lunch with him and the topic of Doreen came up he said, "I think Virginia was the money-earner, the leader, but that she failed to work on the marriage, to invest in it, perhaps because she was too self-centered." This narcissistic need to become the center of attention and to show a lack of understanding of the needs of others is a long-standing personality characteristic of Virginia's and it has contributed to serious difficulties in her interpersonal relationships. Bullough concluded: "I think Virginia made an unfortunate husband, and I think Doreen was an unfortunate wife."

Prince never engaged in sexual excursions outside of either marriage. She told me with pride of her conventional monogamy: "I've had sex with two women in my life, and I was married to each of them." Today, Prince is totally unable to recount the unhappy events basic to Doreen's moving out, initially, to live with the Lowmans. But fidelity is only one issue in a marriage. As best we can judge, Bullough is on target in questioning Prince's capacity for fulfilling the needs of a marital partner. Perhaps Virginia's pervasive narcissism left little energy for providing a loving and supportive relationship with a wife.

Based on what Prince told Stoller at the time, Doreen was especially anxious about Virginia's possible transition to living full-time as a woman. Prince had developed a friendship with a post-operative transsexual, Sherry, and Doreen was not happy about this, believing her to be a bad influence. The marriage grew more troubled, although Doreen had previously been quite supportive of Virginia's transgender behavior, sight-seeing in San Francisco with Virginia, participating in meetings of the Alpha Chapter, and making joint presentations to college classes.

After she left Prince and moved in with the Lowman's, Doreen and Arnold tried to work their problems out, but without success. Both received some counseling from Dr. Stoller, none of which seemed to help. "I loved her a great deal," Virginia told Stoller, "...and that's why it hurt me so deeply when she left." It is interesting to speculate on possible scenarios for Virginia's life had this marriage not only survived, but grown stronger. Would Virginia Prince have begun her full-time transition within a year? We learn from the Stoller interviews that Virginia was deeply hurt by having his wife "just up and walk out on me," and that he loved her very deeply. This was only one of several examples of Prince not comprehending the process of losing a close relationship.

Their sexual relationship and the fractures in the marriage were both complex, based on what we can derive from the Stoller interviews. Virginia characterized Doreen as having conflicts about her own sexual identity, especially in terms of feeling uncomfortable with anything suggesting her possible "latent homosexual feelings." Doreen was described by Stoller as "emotionally exhausted" with her struggles over the possibility of Virginia evolving into a full-time woman. Additionally, Brent, then 19, who was Prince's son from the first marriage, was having serious personal problems, apparently involving drugs, and he had come to live with his father and Doreen. This almost certainly added more stress within the household. It is not clear whether Prince had much energy or insight to assist his deeply troubled son whose mother was living in the Midwest.

During these difficult times, Prince told Stoller that his wife (Doreen) had actually encouraged him "...to have the operation...then we could live together as two women"

(Stoller, #3, p. 19). However, most of the interview in early 1965 suggests that Doreen would not accept such a relationship, even if Virginia had sought it. While Prince had surely entertained the idea of living as a woman, at no time had she ever planned to have genital surgery as Doreen was said to have suggested. At that time, Virginia assumed that within about a month Doreen would make up her mind about remaining in the marriage, or ending it. Doreen moved in to the home of the Lowman's and tried to think through her options.

Doreen obtained a divorce in 1966 and retained more than half of their assets, including the house. Virginia rented a small house in Laurel Canyon. At this time Virginia was 54. She was now entirely alone and without any obligation to other people, except for the son, Brent. At her business, work obligations also ended with the outright sale of Virginia's half ownership of Cardinal Industries in 1968. Now, Virginia Prince was at liberty to live as she pleased, and in June of that year, at the age of 55, she began a new life as a full-time, non-surgically re-assigned woman. The steps leading to this gender transformation have been explained in considerable detail in various issues of Transvestia, especially Volume 100.

*"The whole idea of transvestism
is being your own love object."*

*Virginia Prince*
(Stoller, #17, p. 44)

## CHAPTER 5

# Cross dressing era (1924-1967)

### Age 12 (1924)

The cross dressing experiences of Muriel, Arnold's first feminine name, began with his erotic attraction to high heeled shoes. Who can say precisely what combination of motives led to this attraction? We know that the adolescent Arnold was a lonely lad who felt overlooked within the family, and that he was strongly fearful about any sort of dating relationship. We can only assume that the high heeled shoes were a clearly evident symbol of both the femininity and the love and affection he so strongly sought. One problem was that there were very few pairs of high heeled shoes in his house, as his physician father disapproved of them. Arnold therefore began cutting out pictures of his favorite women's shoes and compiling a small scrapbook which he kept secret. He found the handling of high heeled shoes very sexually arousing and this always led to masturbation and orgasm. However, Prince makes it clear that "I never had the slightest interest in leather or rubber fetishism -- my goal was to look like the best woman I could." The use of more and more articles of clothing together with makeup and a wig were essential to achieve this goal. Therefore, she explained, "I started borrowing my mother's clothes, putting them on secretly, and occasionally went out at night, walking along Wilshire Boulevard... I was scared to death."

Like so many other cross dressers, Arnold's initial erotic fascination with shoes had generalized to other items of feminine attire, culminating over months and years into a full wardrobe, makeup and a wig. Over scores of hours of solitary, secretive practice, she had constructed, piece by piece, skill after skill, the attractive, sexy, woman in the mirror that she wanted to see; for her, it's a reflection that has never lost its erotic power. Virginia stashed her feminine attire in a trunk in her room or in the family garage. After a year or two, she began more bold practice as a young lady-at-large, with trips on buses and window shopping in downtown Los Angeles.

She dates 1929, at age 16 as a time when her cross dressing interests had become "full blown." Her parents had arranged a family vacation to Europe, and aboard a transatlantic ship, young Arnold was urged by a lady passenger to attend the Captain's fancy dress ball as a girl. Aware that this could be seen as a quite unusual, Virginia declined, although "there was nothing in the world I wanted to do more..." (Transvestia, Vol. 100). Was his reluctance to wear a feminine costume, at least in part, indicative of the anticipation of parental disapproval? For the highly secretive Arnold, appearing as a girl may have felt like a dangerous step out of the closet. This incident is one I've heard Virginia recite many times; it clearly meant a lot to her. She reports that at the age of 16 "I had never even heard of transvestism and I certainly didn't know any other cross dressers."

Throughout these teenage years, sexual excitement when cross dressed, together with masturbation and orgasm, were very rewarding to her. Today, she is not hesitant to discuss these sources of pleasure and she has also written in detail about sexual factors associated with transvestism (Transvestia, Vol. 65). "There is hardly any purpose in hiding the erotic aspects of early cross dressing and I had my share of that. Most every dressing session involved an orgasm and sometimes things came to a climax while I was on the street, the excitement was so intense. I'm sure I wasn't in any way unique in that regard" (Transvestia, Vol. 100, p. 7). Looking across her adult life, it's clear that sexual and erotic rewards have been even more important to Virginia than she acknowledged in her Transvestia articles, many of which intellectualize and deemphasize these erotic experiences. This is not surprising, given the intense disapproval of candid sexual discourse in our culture.

On one of her youthful excursions to downtown Los Angeles, Virginia discovered that even while enjoying the display of lingerie and fine women's clothing in the department store windows "...I first realized that there was something more to the dressing thing than just a sexual outlet...it was the beginning point of awareness of the 'girl within' philosophy (that)...came to be the cornerstone of my philosophy' (Transvestia, Vol. 100, p. 8). For her, this was a turning point involving far greater emphasis on the formation of her feminine gender identity.

# *Age 18 (1930)*

Virginia's first presentation of herself, fully dressed, among people who knew him as Arnold was at the age of 18. Here's how Virginia described it. "A very nice lady across the street with children who were my friends through our church suggested that she outfit me as a girl to attend the church Halloween party. I loved doing this, and the following day I dressed again before returning the outfit to her, so I could take some pictures" (Transvestia, Vol.100, p. 7). This was my first picture as Virginia. Following the party a small group of the young people drove to the beach where Virginia enjoyed walking around in the company of many people.

It seems to have required at least ten years for Virginia to progress from a mostly sexual phase of cross dressing to one in which the expression of her feminine gender identity became the most important to her. The social feedback from people who treated her as a woman became very rewarding. In an interview with Dr. Stoller she put it this way: "As a boy at the age of 12, when I'd get all dressed up it was purely an exciting and masturbatory thing. It wasn't until I was in my early twenties when I began to realize that there was something more to it than just putting on dresses and masturbating. All the rest of those years, through two marriages, (even when cross dressed) I was mostly Arnold" (Stoller, #17, p.15). Summing it all up in 1984 she said "I was a traditional TV (transvestite), a classical TV" (Stoller, #28, p. 8).

# Age 30 (1942)

As noted earlier, while Virginia was a laboratory assistant at the University of California Medical School in San Francisco, she became aware of a case presentation in the Psychiatry Department involving a transvestite, soon to be identified as Louise Lawrence. She attended the case presentation and then sneaked a look at the case file, obtaining the address of this individual. At that time, they both lived across the bay in Berkeley. Soon thereafter, Prince telephoned the Lawrence household and explained her desire to meet. This led to Virginia's first conversation with another cross dresser.

It was on the evening of her first meeting with Lawrence that Virginia first used the name, Virginia Prince. "I needed a name," she explained, "and I lived on Prince Street and that's where my last name came from." Significantly, Lawrence served as a role model at that early time in Virginia's life, initially presenting herself during those years as a well-functioning, passable, heterosexual cross dresser. A few years later, Lawrence began living full-time as a non-operative transgender woman, again serving as a role model for Prince.

According to one of the early participants in cross dressing groups in the 1940s, Lawrence played a key role by serving as the hub of an informal communications network of cross dressers spanning California. This word-of-mouth network was based upon addresses given in men's magazines that printed so-called contact ads. Born in 1913, Lawrence successfully transitioned to living fully as a woman in 1944; she died in 1976 (Meyerowitz, 2002). One of her cross dresser friends told me that she had held a job, as Louise, in a downtown San Francisco bank. Beginning in the 1940's,

Lawrence had worked closely with Dr. Karl Bowman of the University of California's Langley-Porter Clinic, Alfred Kinsey, and Harry Benjamin, all of whom were major players in the emerging transgender movement. Virginia Prince could not have chosen a more influential or better connected transvestite fellow-traveler. Later, we shall have more to say about the impact of Prince's new friend.

Over several years, I have asked Prince how she happened to initially select the name Muriel, and then abandon it for Virginia. She told me that there was no special story -- that she simply liked these names. However, upon review of the Stoller transcripts it turns out that while mentioning some of the girls she was attracted to during elementary school, one of her favorites was Virginia Chatham. Perhaps this is just a coincidence; we have no way of knowing. Her abandonment of her given first name, Arnold, in favor of Charles is explained as a choice to adopt the name of her father. But Virginia Prince did not wind up years later thinking of herself as a "psychic transsexual" and as a "woman" simply because of the names she had selected; this was the product of decades of gender role practice, social feedback, a motive to be the best looking woman she could be, and her considerable success in all of these efforts.

During the post-graduate year at the medical center, Virginia arranged to meet the Director of the Langley-Porter psychiatric clinic, the prestigious Dr. Karl Bowman, who essentially told her that transvestism was "...no big deal..." and that she should simply live her life and "be yourself." These words have guided Virginia Prince throughout her life and they have been one of the themes she has used in advising other cross dressers, their wives and transgenderists.

*Virginia visits San Francisco, about 1955*

# Age 34 – 55 (1946 – 1967)

Beginning at age 12, Virginia practiced secretive, occasional cross dressing, mostly at home for over twenty years. Nearly all of this was kept apart from his first wife, Dorothy, especially during the first five or six years of marriage. "Toward the end of my first marriage, we had settled in Los Angeles, and I decided to do a half-woman/half-man costume for the Halloween party at church. I had gone to my parents' house and retrieved one of the long dresses my sister had left there when she got married. I showed my wife, Dorothy, the costume and she was not thrilled, but I had become more bold and confident. I made it clear that I was going to wear this costume and that was all there was to be said." Continuing, she explained, "Soon thereafter, we had a long talk about my cross dressing and she agreed that I could do it whenever I wanted, but not in her presence. She also agreed to buy clothing for me as she didn't want me to take the risk of doing that myself." For the next 18 months, Virginia dressed "on the average…about once every two weeks."

Virginia's son, Brent, had been born in 1946 "…and I took on many motherly duties." Virginia remained married to her first wife, Dorothy, for seven years and "I thought we had a happy family….we moved across town and got a new house in Westwood." (Transvestia, Vol. 100, p. 14). They were divorced in 1951. Several years later, Virginia called upon Dorothy at her home near Minneapolis, and they enjoyed a cordial dinner together. They never met again.

There were nine years between the divorce from Dorothy and Prince's marriage to Doreen Skinner. During that time, in 1955, Virginia began to take female hormones "…for a few years." Her goal was to acquire sufficient breast development to enable some cleavage to be shown, but not to use hormones in a quantity that would interfere with erection and orgasm. These erotic feelings have been highly valued by Virginia throughout her life. She told a friend that she stopped taking these hormones because she was concerned that they might increase her risk for cancer in later years.

During the years between marriages Virginia carried out several ambitious trips to test her skills as a woman in public places. She visited San Francisco for several cross-dressed weekends, typically traveling by train, as Arnold.

*Virginia Prince at the age of 47*

On one of these San Francisco trips, Virginia arranged to meet a woman named Betty who was a friend of the medical school psychologist. Virginia and Betty spent a highly enjoyable evening together that included drinks at the Top of the Mark where they were propositioned by a pair of servicemen. They declined, but Virginia describes this as an especially important evening because she came to realize that she was not just dressing up as a woman, she was "being a woman." Not only that, she was "…sufficiently a woman to be the object of masculine attention in the lounge." She hated having to return home as Arnold when this magical weekend was over. Through these real-life experiences Virginia was progressively functioning with increasing confidence in the role of a woman, and constructing the stronger feminine gender identity that twenty years later would help her to live entirely as Virginia. "During this period I was giving consistent attention to being the best cross dresser that I could be, and to learning all I could about finding acceptance as Virginia in the real world." Throughout this time, Virginia considered herself to be a typical heterosexual, periodic cross dresser. She had never lived as Virginia for more than a few consecutive days.

In the early 1960s, Virginia began to learn of other cross dressers in the Los Angeles area, possibly from magazine articles containing so-called contact ads; often one contact led to another. These contacts and communications among cross dressers led to a series of transvestite get-togethers that took place at the modest home of a Long Beach cross dresser, Johnny Thorn, who was not employed at the time. Virginia told me: "I'll always remember that place because he had an old sofa with a spring sticking out." Typically, not more than six cross dressers would be present for one of these informal discussions. This group never adopted a name. The participants consisted of heterosexual men drawn from all parts of southern California and representing many different occupations and socioeconomic levels. This informality was to change under Virginia's leadership. In her view, it was time to get organized. We are not concerned here with the history of the gay and lesbian movements in the United States, but it may be noted in passing that just ten years earlier one of the first of the important gay rights groups, the Mattachine Society, was founded in Los Angeles. The transgender movement and the gay rights movement developed in parallel, but quite independently, and some of their deepest roots were planted in Los Angeles.

In 1961 Virginia started a support group for cross dressers called The Hose and Heels Club. She mailed invitations to all known cross dressers in southern California, most of them having been subscribers to Transvestia magazine, inviting them to attend a meeting, not cross dressed, and to bring along a pair of pantyhose and a pair of high heeled shoes. Transvestia, the magazine, was founded in 1960 and we'll explain this story later. For the Hose and Heels Club, the idea was that security would be enhanced when they all donned these items at the same time during the meeting. Fortunately, the meeting did not result in any security problems. We must recall that it was not until the late 1960s that the arrest and prosecution of cross dressed men was terminated in southern California and in most parts of the United States. The so-called disguise ordinances had been used for decades, mainly to suppress prostitution by cross dressed males. The initial Hose and Heels meeting was held in a house that adjoined church property in Hollywood. A follow-up meeting was held at the home of one of the Hose and Heels attendees, a dress designer and friend of Prince's. Virginia regards this home meeting as the beginning of the first transvestite organization in history. It led at first to the formation of FPE, The Foundation for Full Personality Expression, and later to a successor organization, Tri Ess, the Society for a Second Self. The initial support group was assigned the name of the Alpha Chapter and Prince began to work energetically to help other chapters become established. Vern and Bonnie Bullough attended the second meeting of the Hose and Heels group, and Bonnie described her impression to her husband this way: "There were 12 or 14 cross dressers in attendance who reminded me of a bunch of young girls at a wedding shower, giggling and acting like teenagers." Prince enforced a no alcohol policy at these meetings.

Throughout the 1960s and the early 1970s, when Prince thought of herself as a periodic cross dresser, Virginia often sought opportunities to live for several days at a time in her feminine mode, apparently passing effectively as a woman.

51

Judging from surveys of cross dressers, these longer excursions were uncommon among periodic cross dressers at that time. One unusual trip enabled Virginia to spend a weekend in San Diego as the "wife" of an Alpha Chapter member who took the part of the "husband" and Virginia enjoyed this very much. They dined out and then danced at one of the city's most fashionable hotels. Presumably, this weekend had been arranged by the wife of the man who escorted Virginia to San Diego; this gentleman was also a cross dresser (Transvestia, Vol. 8).

Although Virginia does not explicitly say so, it seems likely that she may have given some thought to what it would be like to live entirely as Virginia, once her marital obligations ended, in about 1967. At the least, Virginia engaged in several weekend adventures totally as Virginia, passing and perfecting her role as a woman. A detailed history of these different trips is provided in Volume 100 of Transvestia. Looking back, Virginia noted that "…there was nothing in the world I wanted to do more" (Transvestia, Vol. 100, p. 5). By this time, Virginia had her hands full with the operation of a business, the writing and production of Transvestia, and serious difficulties with her son Brent. Additionally, she was also a very active periodic cross dresser and soon she would begin to travel extensively, as Virginia, to visit the new chapters of her national organization.

*"...a bit of fetishism, a bit of narcissism, and a bit of acting..."*

Virginia Prince

## CHAPTER 6

# Transgender era (1968-2002)

## *Age 55*

There were major changes in Virginia's life during these years. Here is how she described the processes of change: "In 1968, I took a very extensive six week trip throughout the United States entirely as Virginia, speaking on radio and television programs, meeting with other cross dressers, and even meeting with police department people." Virginia made this trip without any of her masculine clothing and it was this journey that became the catalyst resulting in her decision to commence living entirely as a woman. Virginia's self-evaluation of this extended opportunity to perfect and test her feminine self-presentation was entirely positive. Each step of the way, each new day, every new challenge, all combined to strengthen her conviction that she was capable of performing very successfully in the role of a woman. This trip was the culmination of many years and many experiences wherein Virginia had done the same thing but for shorter periods of time. She had traveled through the nation and into Canada, by plane, automobile, train, and even aboard ships. Virginia had constructed her own feminine persona, tested it in the real world, and decided to live entirely as a woman.

Continuing the personal history she gave me, "I had returned from a very successful trip and I'd lived for six weeks or so as Virginia without a stitch of men's clothing. I was living in a house in Laurel Canyon and sitting on the patio reflecting on what I had just done, and what I wanted to do in the future. I looked at the door to the street and asked myself: Will Charles (i.e., Arnold) be going out that door in the future, or will it be Virginia?" The decision was to become Virginia Prince and to put aside virtually all of the former life of Arnold Lowman. In Volume 62 of Transvestia magazine, Virginia gives the date of April, 1968 as the commencement of her living full-time as a woman. However, in Volume 100 she marks the date as June, 1968.

One of her most unusual experiences was a nude marathon group therapy session led by psychologist Paul Bindrim in 1968 (Transvestia, Vol. 52, p. 67). Virginia had invited Bindrim to speak at some of the Alpha Chapter meetings and when she learned that he was conducting nude therapy sessions she was eager to participate. Her view was that such a group session would be a unique opportunity, not only for intense emotional expression which she seemed to need very much at that time, but more important, it was a way to test her success in the presentation of Virginia while removing all clothing and revealing her male anatomy. The session began at 4 p. m. on a Saturday in the Palm Springs area. There was considerable opportunity for emotional expression, with Virginia tearfully describing her desire to unload the heavy burden of masculinity and of having to "...make all the decisions." She was reassured that the therapist would make some of her decisions for her. Her nude interactions with others included "...looking in his eyes (that is, a participant's) and then I gently pushed him to sit down and I curled up in his lap and snuggled into his arms. He held me close and gave me a kiss" (p. 72).

This writing is as emotionally explicit as any found in Transvestia. Apparently Virginia felt that something within the context of psychotherapy could be experienced and described with whatever emotional intensity it seemed to deserve. In a real gender inversion, while dealing with a female nude participant, she continued: "I bodily picked her up in my arms and carried her to the couch and told her that she was my daughter" (p. 72). Virginia titled this summary, "My Goal Attained." She meant that this nude session provided an especially clear proof of her feminine gender identity, both as she experienced this, and as she was perceived by others. Hence, her goal had been attained. "For about 20 hours I was as naked as the day I was born but for those same 20 hours I was still Virginia both to myself and to all the rest." She concluded: "I know that I am Virginia, and Virginia is for real. This is the end of the road in the self-acceptance battle..." (p. 79). Going even farther, she finished the article by saying that the nude encounter group not only had allowed her to discard her wig but it had given her "...the final knowledge and assurance of who I am, where I'm at and where I'm going" (p. 82). Femininity, Virginia wrote, was leading to "new experiences, feelings and insights, so why should I change back ..." Referring to her male persona, she promised not to "kill him off" but to hold Charles in reserve "against the day when I may need the more aggressive, sharp and alert strengths of masculinity" (p. 82). Some might reason that Charles has remained very much a part of Virginia, especially when she lurches into an argumentative mode, yet the persona presented to the world has consistently been that of Virginia. At least some of the unusually strong emotion experienced by Virginia in Palm Springs may have been due to the fact that this occurred just a few weeks after she had made the decision to live entirely as a woman. Janis Walworth, consultant-advocate for transsexuals and the wife of a transsexual woman, commented that Virginia's nude therapy weekend "…showed her in an unusual risk-taking situation in which high emotional expression was juxtaposed with her more typical rigidity."

During 1968, she bought a spacious home on a large lot in one of the canyons close to Hollywood. She was now free of nearly all of her business and marital obligations and she had begun living entirely as a woman. At the age of 55 Virginia Prince had been writing and publishing Transvestia magazine for eight years, and while this was a continuing responsibility, Virginia allocated time to enjoy several other challenging activities. These included becoming a glider pilot, owning and flying a powered Ultralite aircraft, acquiring a motorhome and traveling throughout the western states, and taking trips to every corner of the world.

*Virginia became a glider pilot and later flew her own Ultralite*

It is clear that Virginia was never happy just relaxing at home or puttering in a garden. Her greatest delight was in learning some new skills and knowledge, especially in aviation, in exploring the world, and in taking up some challenging new hobby. Some psychologists would describe Virginia as a person with a high motivation for sensation-seeking – that is, one who seeks high levels of arousal and excitement.

It was during this period that Virginia first obtained a United States Passport showing her sex to be Female. For those who like to assign people to categories, she prefers to be designated "...a transgenderist – I live in the feminine gender but I have no desire to change my sex." For Prince, the surgical creation of a vagina for the male-to-female transsexual makes little sense: "...the only thing SRS does is to permit a transsexual woman to have vaginal intercourse with a man, and I'm not into that." She gives little credence to the idea that such surgery is considered by many transsexuals as the ultimate and imperative step in the process of becoming a transsexual woman or man, and that such surgery is critically important to their identity. In many states, including California, it is also recognized as the legal definition of having become a transsexual woman or man. Now and then some gossip is heard alleging that Prince applied for transsexual surgery through the Stanford University program but was rejected. Virginia reports that this is entirely untrue.

Over the years, Virginia has been very outspoken and dogmatic in presenting her opposition to surgical sex reassignment, often going well beyond the simple expression of a personal preference and more into the mode of conducting an ideological campaign. Let's just say she has not shown much acceptance of contrasting opinions on this topic, and it has cost her some friends. But as strong as her views on this may be, she has sustained many close friendships with transgendered women who elected to proceed with surgery. In 1987 an 85th birthday party for Virginia was held at California State University, Northridge, hosted by several of the faculty friends of Virginia and by Sandy Thomas, a long-time friend of hers and the editor-publisher of fantasy stories for transvestites. About 40 cross dressers, along with their wives and friends, watched a slide show portraying Virginia's life.

## Age 88-90 (2000-2002)

Aside from moving to a retirement community, Virginia's life continues much as it has since 1968, when she became a transgender woman. She's in good health, she still travels throughout the nation several times a year and attends many of the major transgender conventions, and she still finds some measure of erotic enjoyment when she catches just the right reflections of Virginia in her mirror.

Virginia explains that it has always been rewarding to express herself as a woman and to be seen as a woman by others, in part, because of deeply held beliefs about her own feminine gender identity, or "girl within." This awareness, however, has not replaced her life-long erotic enjoyment of being "gussied up" to look especially sexy, at least in her own view. She explained it this way. "I think it's as simple as Charles finding Virginia is an attractive woman…a sex object of sorts." At 88, Virginia described herself as "…still entirely capable of sexual arousal and orgasm…" However, at 90 she complained that some of the medication she now must use "…wipes out my ability to keep an erection – perhaps I need some Viagra," she joked.

When asked about the disappointments in her life she has little to say: "I suppose I'd have to say that having gotten a Ph.D. from the University of California, I actually didn't do much with it -- I didn't put it to much use. Maybe my cross dressing was a factor in that, because that required me to be on guard in my early years, it took a lot of psychic energy." When asked if there were any major changes in her life that she would make if she could live it over again, Virginia said the only issue would be whether she'd elect to have gender reassignment surgery "…but I don't think I'd want to do that."

# CHAPTER 7

# Prince-Stoller Interviews

For 29 years, beginning in 1962, Virginia met about twice a month with psychiatrist Robert Stoller who specialized in studies of sex and gender at the UCLA Neuropsychiatric Institute. During the spring of 1962, Virginia had given a lecture at the University of Southern California Medical School and while there she had learned of Stoller's work. She contacted him and an appointment was arranged. Prince appeared as Arnold for their first session, and thereafter, as Virginia.

Robert Stoller was a handsome, affable, political liberal who was one of the first tenure-track psychiatrists hired by the newly established UCLA Medical School, Department of Psychiatry. He was the son of a New Jersey business executive and was the product of a loving and warm family. He had married a charming young woman. His primary professional goal was to earn a reputation as a psychoanalytically-trained sex and gender researcher, and he immediately welcomed Virginia Prince as a research resource. Those who knew Stoller, and I knew both him and his father fairly well, described him as a warm, welcoming and friendly person.

Typically, they would meet for an hour or an hour and one-half every two weeks. Stoller mainly listened, taking the role of the student, while Virginia offered her opinions and

61

interpretations of the questions he posed; she also discussed her personal life in considerable detail, speaking with both a clear focus and a story-telling style. Her verbal essays often seem like mini-lectures, with thoughtful organization and a highly literate and grammatical style. Prince did almost all the talking. One persistent theme persued by Prince was her insistence on clarification of the differences between the words, sex and gender. She insisted that the term, sex, should be biologically defined, while the term, gender, should refer to attributes of masculinity and femininity. Hence, for sex one would speak of male and female, while the words, man and woman, would apply to gender. Stoller used *Sex and Gender* as the title of his first two books. Both Vern Bullough and Richard Green knew Stoller well and each told me Prince deserves the credit for the first useful clarification of these terms, and that in this matter she had much influence upon Stoller.

Stoller described his interviews with Prince as "…something less than psychotherapy, but more than casual conversation." In fact, from the transcripts to be described here, it is clear that the interviews had very little to do with psychotherapy. The only exception was at the time of Doreen's pending divorce, when he offered her a few sessions of marriage counseling.

Stoller's role was to probe Virginia with brief questions aimed at clarification of details and elucidation of meanings of words and pictures, often from the sexual magazines donated by Prince or from her own vivid description of sexually toned experiences. Stoller typically prodded Virginia by saying he didn't understand her, prompting her to elaborate. He'd ask, "Well…help me to understand…I need to get this straight…can you clarify the difference between…" Virginia proved to be a perfect research subject, never tiring of explaining her viewpoints and very willing to reveal a great deal about her own sexual fantasies and her sexual behavior. She was entirely trustful of Stoller, and both knew the rules of confidentiality for these research-based interviews. It was never intended that any of these recorded sessions be used by anyone other than Dr. Stoller, and he assured Prince that her identity would not be revealed. As we noted in the Introduction, all of this changed when Stoller was killed in an automobile accident and the recordings and transcripts were given to Virginia at the direction of Mrs. Stoller.

Stoller was the author of many books and articles about sex and gender, all written from a traditional orthodox psychoanalytic point of view. His outlook was so strictly Freudian that many of his contributions have been discounted by the researchers of today. For the most part, his observations were derived from individual interviews; he rarely met transgendered individuals outside of his medical school office. As part of his continuing research efforts, he had organized an interdisciplinary professional study group that met every second Saturday and included anthropologists, psychologists, and sociologists.

A reading of the Prince-Stoller transcripts reveals Virginia as a very intelligent person with a great skill for analysis of complex interpersonal situations, and for examining her own tangled erotic motivation. She had no difficulty holding her own when the two might disagree on the definition of terms. She was highly organized in her presentation of ideas, and she never tired of explaining her feelings to Dr. Stoller.

Stoller recorded their sessions, initially using reel-to-reel equipment and later, cassette recordings. He selected various segments from them to have transcripts typed with the goal of using them in a future book or article. Stoller did some careful editing of a few of them, but so far as is known, he seldom if ever utilized quotations from the material. His articles and books do, however, contain several thinly disguised descriptions of Virginia. On a few transcripts he penciled in the pseudonym of Philip in place of the name, Charles or Arnold. Exactly how Prince may have influenced Stoller can not be precisely assessed, but the production of this 29 year case history is, in itself, probably the most extensive record of a transgendered person's case history ever to be acquired.

The content of these transcripts, selected by Stoller, offers not only a glimpse into what Virginia had to say about various topics, but more importantly, some private and unguarded revelations of her own erotic and emotional life, and a good deal about her growing-up years. When these sessions began, Prince was 49, married and living in Hollywood as a periodic cross dresser and co-owner of a small business. Volume 14 of Transvestia had just been mailed to a few hundred subscribers.

I have not listened to all of the tape recordings from which the transcripts were made, but I was given access to the transcripts by Virginia. The second interview transcript is dated June 21, 1962 and the final one bears the date of November 24, 1986, the day following Prince's 74th birthday. We don't have the date of the first interview, but was almost certainly in early June, 1962. Keep in mind that all of what we have in the 900 pages of transcripts is what Stoller thought might be most useful to him. These may or may not be representative of the remainder of the non-transcribed sessions.

Early in June, 1962, at their first session, Arnold laid out a very ambitious agenda, explaining his desire to meet with other psychiatrists, to give lectures, and become more involved as an educator within the medical school. Prince's unrealistic and somewhat grandiose expectations were clearly set forth. Stoller explained that some of this could be arranged, but he described the realistic limits of what he could be expected to do. This was essentially a session in which the two individuals were getting acquainted and laying out what they sought from each other. Late in the first interview, Arnold launched into a sweeping and simplistic explanation of the role of femininity in the male as he believed this to be related to most mental disorders: "It is my personal feeling that the presence of femininity in the male individual…is the preeminent problem of psychiatry. I think it accounts for most homosexuality, most alcoholism, transvestism, transsexuality, a great deal of psychosomatic complaints, a lot of neurotic cases and probably a few psychotics…" (Stoller, #1, p.10). Stoller agreed: "Well, you are not the original discoverer of that. You know the psychiatric literature is filled with patients describing this as a possible cause of the things you mention."

Prince had grown up around physicians and he seemed almost too sure of himself in their initial interview when he offered to expand the knowledge of the UCLA psychiatric faculty, if not the entire medical school. He explained his goal to Stoller: "It has been one of the ambitions of my life…to impart some knowledge about this subject (transvestism)…psychiatry, like the man on the street, has largely got the idea that transvestism must be (related to) homosexuality, if not overt, then latent..." (Stoller, #1, p. 7). Whatever else Prince might have been explaining, no matter who the audience, she has invariably given prominence to the fact that the typical transvestite is heterosexual, and that the alleged causal role of homosexuality has been entirely misunderstood by both professionals and by the general public.

This first meeting ended with Arnold asking Dr. Stoller to send him a letter inviting "Virginia Bruce" (i.e., Virginia Prince) to come and be interviewed again. This letter was requested to provide the necessary excuse for Prince to come to UCLA dressed as Virginia which would have been a parole violation stemming from charges brought by postal authorities that will be discussed later. Virginia was aware that such a violation could lead to incarceraton in a federal prison so she didn't want to take an unnecessary risk. During this time, however, Virginia's probation was ended by the order of the sentencing judge, prior to June 21, 1962 which was the date of the second interview.

Stoller inquired about the "rewards" of cross dressing, and in particular the sexual aspects of this. Virginia chose to explain, first, her real-life avoidance of any sex play with other men, and second, a hypothetical example. In real-life, she said she'd had never had "a date" with a man that included any kind of erotic activity. This was not quite correct, for soon thereafter we learn from other Stoller-Prince conversations that she did enjoy going out with a cross dresser who took the role of the man, while Virginia was his cross dressed date, and that this did include some erotic play. At least one such special friend took her to upscale places for lunch and drinks, and later what she described as "mutual masturbation...but never once was there any kind of anal or oral sex...never." These events

66

occurred over several years, often about every six weeks. The male was a cross dresser but always dressed as a man for these erotic sessions. With Stoller, she explained that in a hypothetical encounter with a man who attempted to have sexual relations with her that "I'd be faced with the fact that I simply haven't got what Virginia should have" (Stoller, #2, p. 15). Later, Prince would describe other sexual adventures with men, always emphasizing that no touching of her genitals was ever allowed, and that she never participated in any anal or oral sexual contact. These were boundaries Prince never crossed, although she found kissing, hugging, and affection from a man to be very sexually rewarding. Prince was not shy about revealing this sexually satisfying side of her cross dressing: "I would be dishonest and foolish if I were to try to indicate that (there) was no sexual relationship (in cross dressing)…there is always a relationship, a connection, but every time I have a dress on I don't have an erection (and) I don't have to masturbate" (Stoller, #2, p.17). More than once she explained that in her life as Virginia, "…there is a bit of fetishism, a bit of narcissism, and a bit of acting" (p.18). At other times, Prince becomes more sexually explicit, describing how, in bed, she would enjoy sex role-playing in which his second wife would pretend "…to give me a baby…laying on top of me" (p. 19). The interviewer asked if Virginia might someday wish to have her penis cut off. "No," she explained, "I don't want it cut off for a simple reason…The experience of sex is satisfying. If I were to have (it) cut off I would be unable to have (a) sexual experience." There is much evidence that Prince has always valued her penis as a primary component of her own sexuality, and that the thought of not having this asset is repugnant. This is at the heart of her intense disapproval of gender re-assignment surgery.

While Prince explained that "I wouldn't want the operation..." she also described an intense emotional response to the newspaper reports of the "sex change" surgery of Christine Jorgensen. "At the time it hit the paper, I was sick for three days...literally, my stomach turned over." She continued, "Here was an individual who could do as she pleased (as a woman)...she looked very pretty...Now, I envied that." Stoller asked: "By sick, then, you mean sick with envy?" Virginia replied: "My whole feeling was, my God, if I could only do this" (Stoller, #2, p. 25). When the tumult died down...and I thought about it more...I knew this (sex change) wasn't right – that I wouldn't want to accomplish the end at the price that had to be paid" (p. 25). Prince said then and in her Transvestia Virgin View essays that her goal was to have "the best of both the masculine and the feminine world."

Virginia explained to Stoller the stories she often mentioned in Transvestia, when as a youth she would dress fully as a woman, go to downtown Los Angeles "...for some window shopping, or to a show, (perhaps) eat at a cafeteria, then come home on a bus." These activities were successful, enjoyable, harmless, and seem to have put in place a sense of confidence in assuming the role of a woman. Before long, Virginia would be spending weekends in San Francisco, sometimes with her second wife. She described to Dr. Stoller how all of this contributed to the perfection of feminine mannerisms and the growing ability to speak as a woman in public. As the years passed, her voice deepened and one observer who had known her only as an older women noted that "Virginia never sounded like a woman."

The fear, guilt, and loneliness described by many cross dressers in their early years were also taken up with Stoller.

After extensive public cross dressing, Prince explained, "...just like taking dope, the more times you do it and enjoy it, the harder it is to quit, so you go through years of your life scared to death that somebody will find out...you feel as guilty as hell...men just don't do these things...you're a sissy, a pantywaist, and thinking that maybe I am a homosexual, although I never felt any attraction towards men" (p. 34). This reference to homophobic thinking not only is frequently mentioned to Dr. Stoller, it is also prominent in her Transvestia articles and her lectures and public appearances. Prince concluded session two by explained that "Charles and Virginia...occupy the same house." She gave Dr. Stoller a copy of Volume 7 of Transvestia, explaining that it included an essay on why men cross dress; this essay says virtually nothing about sexual rewards associated with cross dressing.

One of the more pleasant experiences in Virginia's life in 1965 was her enjoyment of taking dancing lessons and attending public dances as Virginia. An out-of-town male friend was visiting Los Angeles and the two had gone out for dinner. Later "...he happened to get a free pass for the Palladium so we went over...and danced all night...(the next day) we drove all around the harbor and he took me to dinner...and I felt very "Virginia" the whole time..." (Stoller, #3, p. 20).

Almost a year later we have transcript #4 based on their December 7, 1965 interview. It must be remembered that while the Stoller-Prince interviews were about twice a month, Stoller only selected 33 of these sessions to be transcribed. At this time, the second marriage was ending. Prince was about to apply for a passport in the name of Virginia Bruce and she feared there would be difficulties; the friendship with her transsexual friend, Sherry, had continued. They attended dances together, as two women and they were occasionally the targets of romantic overtures from men. Virginia enjoyed this attention and accepted some affection from men, but never tolerated even the mention of oral or anal sex, something she considered more appropriate " ...to mammals, other than humans."

She explained to Stoller her skill in selecting clothing to display cleavage and her growing skill in attracting men at dances. In contrast, "as Arnold, I don't think about these events...he doesn't enjoy the anticipation of that...As a matter of fact, the whole thing is somewhat repugnant" (Stoller, #4, p. 16). A bit later in this session she again emphasized the absence of any homosexual feeling and stressed instead the importance to Virginia of "...not having to be the aggressive person...the desire to be the recipient, to be made over, to be taken care of, and to take the passive-feminine position" (p. 16).

In December, 1965, after interviewing Virginia for three years, Robert Stoller dictated for his own records the following description of Virginia's appearance. She was 53.

*"It's worth describing Virginia's appearance today which is typical of the way she usually looks: A light brown wig which is not startling but well kept, dangling silver earrings, pancake makeup, sharply red but not extravagant lipstick. On her neck, a necklace made of three strands of large silver balls, pretty garish when taken with all the rest of her appearance, then a V-cut dress out of which peeked the pushed-up bits of breast*

*tissue looking like an old woman's breasts being shown when they shouldn't be with her brassiere showing and the straps showing, the inner side of the two shoulder straps of her dress; the dress, the upper part of it where her bosom is huge and the largeness is increased by a whole bunch of white flowery patterns on a navy blue background, the lower part is just the navy blue. When she sits with her legs crossed you see up the outside of her thigh quite a long distance, it's not particularly attractive, her knees are bony and her legs although not masculinely muscled are not at all like a woman's; her arms have the muscular contour of a man's, they are very smooth and soft skinned though on her forearms they are darker brown while the upper part is light. I didn't really notice her shoes except that they were high heeled. The overall impression is that if this were in fact a woman, no woman of her age and appearance should show so much of herself and I would think there was something severely wrong in the degree of exhibitionism being revealed"* (Stoller, #4, p. 23-24).

# CHAPTER 8

# Transvestia Magazine

*"I have...dealt with the whole subject of cross dressing more deeply, more thoroughly and more usefully than anyone else in this country or elsewhere."*

Virginia Prince
*(Transvestia, Volume 100, p. 117)*

This self-congratulatory statement should not be discounted as boastful or self-aggrandizing. The fact is that Dr. Virginia Prince has written more extensively about transvestism than just about anyone else. Transvestia was founded, edited, published, financed and distributed by Virginia Prince beginning in 1960, expressly for cross dressers. It was a totally non-sexual magazine. About six issues a year were published, and one hundred editions were produced prior to Prince's retirement as editor in 1980. This little magazine is an invaluable historical account of the development of the transgender movement in the United States and to a more limited extent, in Britain and the Scandinavian countries. In addition to telling of the development of many of the chapters of Tri Ess, often including some early pictures of the members,

Transvestia also traces the development of the ideas of Virginia Prince along with much information concerning her personal life.

It was through Transvestia that Virginia Prince helped to facilitate the development of networks of communication and the formation of support groups for transvestites at a time when this had never been attempted by anyone. In my view, Virginia knew exactly what she was doing as she built an international organization, nourished it, and saw it evolve in many ways. There is one other aspect of Transvestia that is unique. This magazine is a rare example of a publication conceptualized and presented entirely to heterosexual periodic cross dressers, despite the fact the editor and several of her co-editors wound up living full-time as women.

As noted previously, the story of Transvestia began when a small group of southern California cross dressers came to know each other, probably through ads appearing in contact magazines. The idea to begin a newsletter called Transvestia originated from discussions among the Long Beach cross dressers who had been meeting now and then, quite informally, at Johnny Thorn's house in Long Beach during the early 1950s. Selection of the name, Transvestia, should probably be credited to Thorn, who later claimed that Virginia "stole it;" the facts of this remain unclear. The first attempt to publish a newsletter called Transvestia was a mimeographed set of unbound pages consisting mainly of short articles about cross dressing together with some comments from various members of the Long Beach group. There is a good deal of substance and thought shown by these early essays and letters. Joanne Meyerowitz (2002) has pointed out that one of the first essays attempted to clarify the

74

heterosexual status of transvestites, a theme that would be restated many time in future editions of Transvestia magazine.

In 1952 two extensive mimeographed editions were produced, mostly under the editorial guidance of Thorn, with several contributions from Virginia, who sometimes wrote using her earlier name, Muriel. The original set of editors and writers seem to have abandoned this project after the first two editions. Then, in 1960, Virginia, along with a second member of the Long Beach group, decided to send out letters to all the cross dressers they could identity, at most a few dozen, asking them if they'd like to subscribe to a magazine for transvestites. About twenty-five or thirty individuals became the initial subscribers, and Virginia and a small staff began publication. The initial idea was to have the magazine printed by another cross dressing friend located in Nashville, Tennessee, but this arrangement never proved workable. While Virginia advertised five or six issues a year, the pace was sometimes a little behind the calendar, especially when her foreign travel was underway. Several times, when she was away on long trips to every part of the world, Virginia assembled an entire edition of photographs without much written content (for example, see Transvestia, Vol. 58). Across the entire one hundred issues, the quality of the photographs is poor, even taking into account the modest quality of inexpensive offset printing of that time. This seems unfortunate in view of the highly visual dimension of transvestism. The purposes of Transvestia were printed on the inside of the cover and included the following:

> *...to provide a center where people interested in this field may gather*

*...to provide opportunity for the expression of opinion and
the sharing of ideas and experiences*

*... to better understand this facet of human
behavior*

*... to provide information about Transvestites and
Transvestism*

*... to gather and disseminate information*

*... to promote and assist in the conduct of
research*

*... to further the understanding of "this
problem" by various professionals*

Following the statement of purposes, the editor supplied
a concluding rationale for the magazine linking the acquisition
of knowledge to personal understanding and self-acceptance,
leading to greater peace of mind and happiness. This
concluded: *"Unhappiness, loneliness and fear have too long
been the lot of Transvestites. It is to be hoped that Transvestia
can help to convert these into peace, togetherness and
relaxation"* (Transvestia, Vol. 6).

Following the two mimeographed versions of
Transvestia, the magazine was published as booklet measuring
6 by 8 1/2 inches, in black and white with color used for some
of the photographs in the early years. Thankfully, this
experiment with color did not last long. Most of the issues
contain about 84 to 96 pages and were printed offset, the least
expensive procedure. The covers of the initial four issues used
amateur art work and are quite dark and unattractive. These

portray a cross dressed man sitting at a dressing table applying makeup. At first, the text was prepared on a typewriter, but soon a word processor was utilized.

The statement of purposes was written nine years before New York City's Stonewall event which was a turning point in how gays and lesbians were treated by police, and that subsequently contributed to the elimination of laws restricting cross dressing in public. The fear and loneliness noted by Prince in her list of purposes were sustained not only through lack of public knowledge about transvestism, but also by the very real prospect of being arrested for nothing more than appearing cross dressed in public. The pages of Transvestia contain many examples of such arrests, fines, and brief time in jail, often without formal charges being filed. Cross dressers who clipped newspaper articles describing the arrest of their fellow transvestites were able to compile scores of such articles and a collection of these news reports, many of them openly ridiculing the arrested cross dresser, may be seen in the Virginia Prince Collection, in the Special Collections Department of the Oviatt Library at California State University, Northridge. Prince collected many of these articles and so did Louise Lawrence and other transvestites. The papers of Louise Lawrence are at the Kinsey Institute. The first editorial office of Transvestia was in a small room on the premises of Prince's jointly-owned Cardinal Industries on Pico Boulevard in Los Angeles. From time to time various persons assisted with the business side and acknowledged correspondence, but Virginia held tight control over the editorial process.

*Issue 5 featured the first of the cover girls*

Volume 6 included a brief description of Prince's first research questionnaire. This was later elaborated and it culminated in an important publication by Virginia and psychologist Peter Bentler (Prince & Bentler, 1972) of descriptive material about transvestites that was widely quoted in psychology and sociology textbooks. Prince also states that a

UCLA sociology doctoral student drew heavily upon her data in the preparation of an article that was well received (Buckner, 1970).

The use of a cover girl was initiated in issue five and continued through about Volume 50. Potential cover girls were asked to supply several photographs and a personal history, and they were requested to pay for the printing of their page of photos. This was only one of the devices Prince used to enhance the modest income generated by the magazine, which was never much of a money-maker. The honor of being the first cover girl went to Annette who described herself in an extensive personal history and provided eight pictures illustrating various lady-like poses. We are told that she was a 28 year old married business manager with one child, living comfortably in Idaho, and that her interest in cross dressing began in very early childhood. As with Virginia, her earliest fascination was with high heeled shoes. After marriage, Annette revealed this shoe fetish to her wife "...who suggested that we buy a pair of heels for my own to be worn whenever I desired at home." Annette apparently experienced considerable conflict, depression and guilt leading to seeking help from a psychiatrist who encouraged her to allow Annette to be expressed. This guidance provided some relief. Annette added: "Still I think that if I should wake up some day and find Annette gone, painlessly as it were, and with a still normal sex drive left, I would doubtless be better off mentally and have fewer problems."

This fetishistic-like dependence of sex drive upon cross dressing is expressed more directly by Annette than is revealed in many of the personal histories published in Transvestia. In this magazine sexual arousal is often a muted or thinly veiled sub-theme, often described as "emotional arousal" although occasionally Virginia used sexual motivation as the main topic of her feature editorial, Virgin Views (see Volume 65). Occasionally the word masturbation is used in personal stories but most of these accounts simply refer to being "aroused." Virginia had good reason to soft-pedal comments concerning sex and cross dressing, for it was very important to conform to the unpublished criteria of the postal authorities who, for many decades up to the 1970s were determined to intercept and eliminate "obscene" material from the mail. These authorities considered virtually anything pertaining to human sexual behavior to be pornographic, including the topic of birth control, sex education, and even sexual anatomy. The Transvestia subscribers were probably relieved to read Virginia's announcement in Volume 6:

**"FLASH...IMPORTANT....READ CAREFULLY...**
**TRANSVESTIA HAS BEEN EXAMINED**
**BY POSTAL INSPECTORS AND HAS**
**NOT BEEN FOUND TO BE UNMAILABLE."**
(Transvestia, Vol. 6, p. 62)

Transvestia may have been "cleared" but Virginia was not. This notice in Transvestia was the first announcement of the serious investigation and subsequent federal prosecution brought against her by postal authorities in 1962. This unpleasant action is described in Chapter 12.

From the outset, Virginia included information in Transvestia of practical value and interest to her readers, such as a list of other magazine articles featuring information or pictures of transvestites. Most issues also included a "person to person" page listing only the state and first name of subscribers seeking to correspond with other transvestites. No post office

80

box number was printed, so for an initial contact, those seeking pen pals would have to arrange to have their mail forwarded through Virginia's office.

Other regular sections included:

*... long fiction articles sometimes spanning more than one issue*

*... extensive essays by Susanna Valenti (Susanna Says), a New York City cross dresser*

*... personal cross dressing histories*

*... letters to the editor along with Virginia's comments*

*... legal news and notes*

*... book reviews*

*... a section devoted to the interests of wives of cross dressers*

*... advertisements of items for sale to transvestites. Virginia offered her own small line of pads, bras, and a few other items, none of which seemed to have endured as commercial products.*

Susanna Valenti, a married New York City businessman and adventurous cross dresser contributed extensively to Transvestia for many years. She had a very cooperative wife and Susanna was a very inventive and entrepreneurial transvestite who also wrote with sparkle and vitality, always encouraging other cross dressers to take some reasonable risks and join in the fun of transvestism. In addition to being one of the first important contributors to Transvestia and the originator of the first convention for cross dressers, she proposed the establishment of a school for transvestites, and offered her resort property in the mountains as a meeting place or retreat for her transvestite friends. Valenti was a powerful role model as the transvestite-on-the-move, very actively out-in-public as Susanna whenever and wherever she pleased. All of this was occurring at a time when many of the Transvestia subscribers remained locked in a "closet," seldom if ever venturing out in public. Susanna's wife, Marie, was the owner of a well-known wig salon in New York City. After many years as a periodic cross dresser, like Louise Lawrence and Virginia Prince, Valenti announced in her Transvestia column a plan to commence living full-time, without surgery, as Susanna. It is not clear whether she ever did live full-time as a woman; Virginia believes she did not. When health problems required more of her time she stopped writing for Transvestia and lost contact with Virginia.

Virginia Prince wrote a detailed but unrevealing personal history for her final issue as Editor of Transvestia, Volume 100. We learn more about her foreign travels than most other topics. Prince sold the magazine and certain Tri Ess assets and responsibilities to Carol Beecroft of Tulare, California, founder of the organization, Mamselle, but within two years Transvestia was a thing of the past. Prince had transferred to Beecroft both the responsibility for Transvestia and for most of the operations of Tri Ess. Perhaps because all of this demanded more time than Carol had anticipated, she subsequently gave the responsibility for the organization over to a new set of officers, based in Houston, and led by the husband and wife team of Jane and Mary Fairfax. They have continued to nurture and facilitate the growth of Tri Ess, and Virginia expresses the highest respect and gratitude for their effectiveness. Transvestia was not re-established, but in its place Femme Mirror appeared about twenty years ago and it has been published regularly ever since.

According to Prince, the mailing list for Transvestia had never reached one thousand. In the mid-1990s, Virginia sold part of her remaining supply of Transvestia and some remaining publication rights to Sandy Thomas of Sandy Thomas Publications. In 2000 she sold four sets of Transvestia and various photographs and personal papers to the Rikki Swin Institute in Chicago, where a Virginia Prince room is maintained. Prince's Transvestia files and manuscript materials were given to the Special Collections Department of the University Library at California State University, Northridge.

# CHAPTER 9

# Revolt of the Alpha Chapter

In her efforts to build a national organization of cross dressers, Virginia initially named her group the Foundation for Personality Expression (FPE). Much later, as explained in Volume 91of Transvestia the organization was re-named the Society of the Second Self, or Tri Sigma (later, Tri Ess). This national organization absorbed the chapters of the earlier association, FPE. The original chapter was the Alpha group in Los Angeles. Typically, the meetings of this chapter included a professional speaker, a discussion of chapter business such as the acceptance of new members, and a few comments about how the expenses of the group ought to be paid. Most of the initial meetings were held in private homes, but later it proved more satisfactory to meet regularly at a downtown motel.

In conducting an Alpha Chapter meeting, Prince left no one wondering who was in charge. An early member describes her as "...entirely autocratic...she did not allow others to participate in interviewing new applicants nor did we vote on them...she was dogmatic in her style, argumentative and a know-it-all." Here is how she appeared to one of the early Alpha Chapter members.

*"Virginia was very dominant in the meetings...it was her club...she wouldn't allow democratic procedures...Gloria, one of the earliest members of Alpha, confronted Virginia about this and she said: 'That's the way it's going to be.' Virginia insisted on doing all of the interviewing of prospective members. This was much resented, but she wouldn't change this practice. She also insisted that only she was in charge of selecting the new members. She had very rigid rules about being heterosexual and about being a cross dresser and not a TS...these were good rules, but now and then she'd let a clinker into the club...someone who actually was a prospective transsexual."*

*"Virginia was always looking for a way to get rich quickly, and that doesn't work...she was pushing the sales of dried foods for survival purposes, and later, the sales of gold and silver through a friend who was her broker. When the members found out she had given him the mailing list with the men's names and addresses, they were furious. This is one of the main things that led to the break off of the Alpha people, and a year later, the formation of the Crossdressers Heterosexual Intersocial Club (CHIC). Virginia had resigned from the Alpha chapter during a very angry confrontation at a meeting about the mailing list. Virginia was especially attacked by Sandy (not Sandy Thomas) who later became a TS"* (Personal communication to RFD, 2002).

Whatever acerbic or overbearing behavior Virginia may have shown at these meetings must have resulted in a widely felt resentment. There seems to have been nearly unanimous discontent with Virginia's leadership style. The Alpha Chapter members subsequently reorganized with little or no change in membership except that Virginia was to be neither a leader nor a member. CHIC continues to exist, as does a new Alpha Chapter, each holding monthly meetings in southern California. As with many transgender support groups, the monthly turn-out for dinner meetings averages about twenty to thirty members along with four or five wives.

# CHAPTER 10

# Organizations and Leaders

Very possibly, Virginia Prince foresaw the immediate impact Transvestia would have as a channel of communication among cross dressers throughout the world. This little magazine was an international stimulus for networking and social organization, much like we see on the internet today. Not only could the cross dressing subscribers communicate with a sympathetic editor like Virginia, they could also place person-to-person ads inviting correspondence with other cross dressers. Even more important, Transvestia taught the cross dressers of the world how to organize and operate local support groups, and showed that this could be done without any harmful consequences. Virginia urged local groups to form and then affiliate with her own national organization, FPE (The Foundation for Full Personality Expression, also known as Phi Pi Epsilon). FPE was later renamed Tri Ess (Society for the Second Self). The plan to form what came to be FPE was laid out in Volume 13 of Transvestia. Of course, it was required that the new sorority chapters accept the basic tenets of Virginia's organization.

While most of the organization's rules and regulations are not controversial, two have become very contentious. Virginia had felt from the beginning of FPE that it must be a group dedicated to serve the heterosexual cross dresser and that being gay should be a disqualification. The most important reason for this rule, explained Virginia, was that "...wives can't be drawn into a support group that includes gay men." Some would argue that this is not true. A second source of conflict involves whether so-called surgically re-assigned transsexuals should be allowed to participate. Prince has stuck to her guns, saying "no" on both issues while reasoning that a surgically reassigned transsexual would offer the worst possible role model as perceived by the wives of heterosexual cross dressers. She apparently saw no contradiction in the fact that she, the founder of FPE and later Tri Ess, had been living as a woman since 1968. Because of these membership rules, several chapters of FPE broke away from the national organization and formed so-called "open groups" that welcomed cross dressers, gays, and transgenderists regardless of sexual orientation, sexual reassignment, or biological sex.

The Alpha Chapter, in Los Angeles, was the flagship group founded by Virginia. The second group was the Beta chapter, based in Madison, Wisconsin, and headed by Fran. "It grew and thrived over several years," said Virginia, "but gradually lost membership and I don't believe it now exists." Virginia recalled that "...in the early years, somebody accused me of skimming off dues money for my personal use, so I nominated Fran to become the Treasurer and sent the checkbook to her -- that put an end to that complaint."

Chicago organized the Chi chapter and for many years this was led by Naomi Owen who continues to be an active Tri Ess member spanning more than 40 years. Her leadership led to the establishment of the Be All You Can Be Weekend event that is now in its 19th year, and that has consistently attracted over one hundred participants to an annual get-together. For many years, the convention moved annually from Chicago, to Detroit, to Cleveland, to Cincinnati, and to Pittsburg. Across the 19 years, they have moved from one of the most run-down motels in Ann Arbor, Michigan, to first-rate hotels in all of these cities.

An effort was made to initiate a Tri Ess chaper in Cleveland, but Virginia's insistence upon her "heterosexual cross dressers only" policy threw this off course. Instead, an independent group, Paradise Club, was formed and this flourished for several years.

The Gamma chapter was established in Boston and included the membership of both Merrissa Sherrill Lynn, founder of the International Foundation for Gender Education (IFGE), and Ariadne Kane, founder of Fantasia Fair and other transgender activities. Virginia is appropriately proud of the many contributions of both Merrissa and Ariadne. Virginia is especially pleased to reflect upon the continued success of Boston's Gamma chapter: "This has been an especially important chapter because of all that Merrissa and Ariadne have done. It's not just my footprints that are left behind, but also those of Merrissa and Ariadne Kane."

In 1987, at the first national convention of IFGE, Merrissa Sherrill Lynn proposed the establishment of an annual award to be given to a person who had made exceptional contributions to the transgender community. Called the Dr. Virginia Prince Outstanding Service Award, the awardees have been as follows:

1987   *Virginia Prince*
1988   *Merrissa Sherrill Lynn*
1989   *Ariadne Kane*
1990   *Sister Mary Elizabeth*
1991   *Betty Ann Lynd*
1992   *Naomi Owen*
1993   *Carol Beecroft*
1994   *Ellen Summers*
1995   *Yvonne Cook-Riley*
1996   *Sheila Kirk*
1997   *Eve Burchert*
1998   *Jamison Green*
1999   *Phyllis Randolph Frye*
2000   *Jane Ellen and Mary Francis Fairfax*
2001   *Jane Fee*
2002   *Holly Boswell*
2003   *Alison and Dottie Laing*

In Detroit an independent transgender group, Crossroads, was formed which continues to have an active membership. This group had also considered an affiliation with Tri Ess but there was objection to the "heterosexual cross dressers only" rule. While describing this, Virginia emphasizes that she is well aware of the strong objection that has been voiced about this rule, and that this has hurt the growth of Tri Ess. But she concludes: "Look...Tri Ess is the largest, oldest, and best organized group for cross dressers in the world." Few will argue about this.

Throughout the nation, other groups came and went, growing rapidly, then falling by the wayside as key leaders initially took responsibility, and then went their own way. As this is written, about two dozen Tri Ess Chapters are "in formation."

Virginia Prince participated directly in the establishment of the Beaumont Society in England. While on a trip there to deliver a paper at a professional meeting, she met with several cross dressers who were interested in starting a support group. Several of these individuals were subscribers to Transvestia. They settled on the general idea of forming an English group, to be called the Beaumont Society. After presenting her paper the following day, Virginia was asked for an interview by a reporter for The Observer, an important British newspaper. She agreed, requesting that the article include a notice of the formation of the Beaumont Society with a contact address. This resulted in an immediate advertisement of the new group which got off to a running start. "It's still thriving," Virginia added, "although it's no longer an affiliate of Tri Ess."

Through the initiative of a Swedish cross dresser, Annette, who met with Virginia in the United States, there was established the FPE of Northern Europe, a cross dressers support organization with chapters in Norway, Sweden, Denmark, and Finland. Two years ago they celebrated their 20th Anniversary and invited Virginia to come as the guest of honor.

Several Tri Ess Chapters have been established in Canada, and Virginia also takes responsibility for the selection of the Seahorse as the symbol and name of the cross dressers organization active in Australia and New Zealand. This was an independent group. Smiling, Virginia added: "So, you can see, this Johnny Appleseed planted some seeds and helped some groups get started."

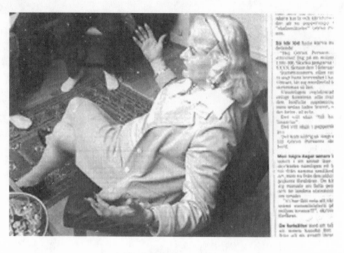

*Virginia was invited to help celebrate the 20<sup>th</sup>*
*Anniversary of the Scandinavian cross dressers group.*
*This photo is from a newspaper article describing the event.*

The successful leadership of Prince in assisting the formation of these support groups and national organizations is apparent, and she regards this as among her most significant contributions. One thing that has been required to accomplish these organizational goals has been a singleness of purpose and a sustained and determined drive toward clear goals. One of her long-time friends, Jane Fee, a former military officer who has lived as a transgendered woman for many years brushed back her shoulder length silver hair and described her friend this way: "She's a fantastic person! She has tenacity in working with transgendered people and organizations. I also find her a nice person to be with. Perhaps she hangs on to some beliefs as always being true, but it's been beneficial to have a person who is very stable and who sticks to her guns. I've found her to be very kind." Fee's own transgender experience began much like Virginia's, at the age of 14; her transition to living full-time as a woman, however, did not occur until about fifty years later.

Others who have known Prince mix praise with some less complimentary observations. One said: "Virginia has tried to observe women, but in many ways she didn't really learn from these observations. Some of her body language is quite masculine. She's very intelligent and very assertive, but she often ignores the counsel of others, and she has to be at the center of attention. It's important that she's given cross dressers a greater sense of belonging." Another long-time friend who has great respect for Virginia said: "She is one of the most masculine transgendered persons I've ever met."

A transgender counselor noted: "Virginia places a great value on her own penis, and this may have caused her to misunderstand the many motives for gender-reassignment surgery, which she opposes so strongly. I consider her homophobic, and perhaps that's due to the era when she grew up. One thing for sure: She has very definite ideas about how a transgendered person should present themselves, but sometimes she fails to meet her own standards."

In recent years, there have been several organizations dedicated to the broad topic of legal and social rights of transgendered persons. For the most part, Prince has not taken an active part in these efforts. She told me: "I never was much involved in the transgender civil rights movements, other than my own advocacy efforts. The organizations supporting this have mainly been in the East. I believe they have accomplished quite a bit."

When asked about national leaders of the transgender movement, Virginia singled out Phyllis Frye who has specialized in legal issues, and her fellow Texans, Linda and Cynthia Phillps, who managed the Texas T Party for many years. Jane Fee, Alison Laing and Sister Mary Elizabeth are also close friends, and there are few within the transgender organizations in America who have not somehow been touched by Virginia Prince.

*Susanna and Virginia*

## CHAPTER 11

# Theory: The Girl Within

In what may be a considerable over-statement, Susanna Valenti wrote that "...our concept of the girl-within is still the closest thing to heaven that the human mind may conceive" (Transvestia, Vol. 100, p. 4). Ms. Valenti was not one to avoid hyperbole. While the idea of a "girl within" may not be quite as close to heaven as she would assert, the concept remains at the core of Virginia Prince's thinking about the origins of gender identity and the concept of gender identity is at the core of understanding transgender behavior. Prince's early lectures to medical school students and service clubs, beginning in 1962, were always titled: *Sex and Gender*. She was one of the first to insist on a clear distinction between these terms. One unusual thing about Prince's "girl within" is that her view of the origin of gender identity is set forth as a biological predisposition, although Prince always played this down. She has always given greater emphasis to learning factors and the so-called social construction of gender identity, rather than to theories of a biological predisposition. It is possible that Virginia was much impressed with the work of John Money and his associates (e.g., Money & Ehrhardt, 1972) that emphasized the social construction of gender identity among intersex persons.

Virginia Prince has written extensively concerning possible explanations for cross dressing and one theme that carries through much of this writing is the concept of a girl within. Virginia credits her fellow Transvestia writer, Susanna Valenti with the origination of this concept although it is impossible to sort out what Valenti contributed from Prince's subsequent elaborations. It is clear that Susanna Valenti invented the term. One difficulty with the girl within theory as an explanation for cross dressing is that it is impossible to pin down precisely what is meant by "experiencing" this girl within. One of the clearest attempts to set forth what is meant by this is given in Prince's book, *Understanding Cross Dressing* (1976). She wrote:

*"...in every male there is buried within a complete "girl." This "girl" consists of the aggregation of all those potentials and possibilities, behaviours and yearnings that are part of his birthright but which society says he must*

*not have, express, do, enjoy, manifest, experience or use"* (p. 12).

Hence, the girl within is a set of "...potentials and possibilities, behaviors and yearnings..." presumably somehow maintained in the brain. Prince reasons that these feminine potentials exist parallel to a set of masculine potentials, the boy within. In males, the masculine potential and behaviors are expressed while the feminine potentials and behaviors are suppressed because of cultural demands to display gender behavior in conformity to one's sex, at least in biological males. Hence, these feminine potentials are said to remain dormant until some sort of releasing or energizing experience happens, usually in the early years of the transvestite-to-be. This boils down to some sort of cross dressing episode, however that may occur. Meanwhile, in the male, the masculine potentials or the "boy within" become progressively stronger as part of the process of learning the skills essential to behavior as a boy or a man in a particular culture. Prince never successfully explained why some boys develop into cross dressers and others who may have had similar "releasing" experiences do not.

In the cross dresser, Virginia observed that something unusual must have occurred, typically without any special effort on the part of the young boy or man. The idea here is that some sort of "special event" taps into the feminine potentials, possibilities, behaviors and yearnings that are central to the girl within. This special event is one in which the male is, at least in part, dressed as a woman, thereby experiencing his previously unrecognized girl within. Prince put it this way: "Now essentially the only difference between FPs (Females Personators, or cross dressers) and any other heterosexual male

99

is that, due to some one of the events mentioned previously, he has 'discovered,' or made contact with his girl within. (This is an) …integral part of his own humanness, (and) that discovery is perceived as being 'good' and good things are sought out again and again" (Prince, 1976, p. 13). Prince reasons that it is biology that is at the base of this feminine potential, or "girl within," but that actual experience in life must act as a releaser to bring forth the special pleasure that sustains subsequent feminine behavior. Hence, as seen by Prince, it is the girl within who, upon being "released," provides the motivational force for the entire process of becoming a male cross dresser.

The forces that have prevented a boy or a man from discovery of these feminine potentials are said to consist of the cultural rules and demands supporting a rigid division between males and females, and also, the demand that one's expression of a gender role be in conformity with his or her biological sex. Prince reasons that it is the rigidity of our culture that must be overcome by a "special event" allowing the male to find the already existing "girl within." She wrote, "I firmly believe that cross dressing is a natural by-product of a culture that divides the total humanity of its citizens up into two so widely different ways of living as is done in western societies." She explained, *"The basic motivation behind cross dressing ... is to be able to recapture some of one's own total humanity through bringing one's 'girl within' into real time and three-dimensional reality"* (Prince, 1976, p. 26).

Prince goes on to explain that the special event in which the boy or the man cross dresses is usually something like a Halloween party, a skit, a mock wedding, or a "…pantie or slip experience." Having developed the main outline of the girl within theory, Prince turns somewhat briefly to sexual rewards and masturbation and orgasm as contributing factors. These are regarded as important added factors but they are accorded secondary status as either causative variables or rewards that help to sustain cross dressing. Virginia's own history of sexual arousal and orgasmic satisfaction associated with cross dressing episodes together with her extensive knowledge of the history of many other cross dressers have provided a basis for her examination of sex as a factor in cross dressing. This has been extensively discussed in her Virgin Views essay in Volume 65 of Transvestia. Here she offers an off-the-cuff estimate that "95%" of all cross dressers will trace at least a part of their cross dressing history to the pleasurable excitement of sexual arousal and orgasm. It was certainly true in her history across many decades. She adds: "The reason this is not discussed more openly is just due to the fact that in our culture it's not considered appropriate to say much about masturbation, orgasm, and so forth."

Taking up another major explanatory theme, Virginia has also strongly emphasized that one of the important rewards for cross dressing is relief from the demands of the masculine role. These demands are described as difficult to bear and through becoming a woman, even temporarily, a valued source of relief is derived. Prince has described the transvestic excursion into femininity as a kind of "vacation" from the demands of masculinity. If you have ever seen Virginia outline her views and defend them in a vigorous debate you would not think she was shy about allowing some masculine characteristics to add strength and color to her speaking style. But nonetheless, the theme of needing a vacation from performing in the masculine role is one of the most important explanations for cross dressing that Virginia has put forth. In my view, this might be related to her historic quest to measure up to the standards of her highly successful father, ever looking to this son to grow taller, get the top grades, win his cross-country high school races, succeed in a prestigious college, and earn a Ph.D. Perhaps some of these very legitimate objectives came to be a heavy burden for Virginia, especially if it is true that her father was, in fact, unrewarding and disappointed with Virginia, as Stoller speculated.

The idea of role relief is one of four concepts used by Prince to explain transvestism to the public or to anyone writing her for an explanation. In an undated publication, believed to have originated in about 1960 or 1961, *An Introduction to the Subject of Transvestism, or Femmiphilia (cross dressing)* (parentheses in the original title), she begins with a contrast between cross dressers and homosexuals. Her initial goal is to eliminate the erroneous idea that the cross dresser is gay. Next, a set of major incorrect explanations are outlined and dismissed, since they are said to be off target. These are: a) wanting a girl and bringing a boy up as a girl; b) keeping a boy in dresses; c) punishing a boy by making him wear a dress; d) inadequate father figure; e) taking refuge in femininity to overcome masculine demands. Prince then offers four "other and deeper reasons" for transvestism:

*1. The need to acquire virtue and experience beauty.*

"Modern man idealizes womankind and makes her the repository of all that is good, true and desirable...this goodness and virtue is not expressed in masculine attire -- it is out of place, but in feminine attire it is in order. In such clothing they can experience beauty and its satisfactions, and symbolically identify with their love object, a woman."

102

*2. The need for adornment and personality expression.*

"Men's clothing is in general, dark, heavy, coarse and plain. It is almost a uniform in that there is little opportunity to vary from the crowd in color, cut or style. Some men find they can fulfill their natural desires by entering into the feminine world of color, fabric, decoration and design."

*3. Relief from the requirements of masculinity.*

"Occasional abandonment of the masculine for the feminine allows the femmiphile (cross dresser) a relaxation from these demands since the feminine role is ideally a passive, accepting, non-demanding one. There is no relaxation comparable to becoming another person, particularly of the opposite gender." The male is said to be restricted in the expression of his "true self" while in masculine attire.

*4. Relief from social expectancy.*

"We are always having to 'live up' to our own developed image... Once in awhile we would like to 'be' another person with a different set of (social) expectations. Most people cannot get away from themselves -- the femmiphile, as his feminine self, can."

While some of these four points have been long advocated by Virginia as important reasons for cross dressing, the way they are presented and their simplistic quality suggest this booklet was little more than a propaganda effort. Prince adds that cross dressing often begins in adolescence, and that it is not likely to change with psychotherapy. She emphasizes that the man is "...seeking personality expression and freedom

103

for the feminine aspect of his being...The male should be entitled to emancipation and freedom of expression just as much as the female." She points out that most femmiphiles "...do not come out and admit their interests. Due to fear of ridicule and false accusations of homosexuality, they keep it a secret." Prince concludes, pleading that we should all become "...more tolerant and understanding of our fellows." This rare document does not give the author's name, but it was definitely written and published by Virginia Prince. The most obvious omission is any mention of sexual rewards as vitally significant in the history of most cross dressers, as documented by all researchers over the past century, and as clearly acknowledged elsewhere by Prince. At the least, this eight page pamphlet gives us a clear understanding of Prince's effort to desexualize transvestism and to position the topic as attributable to identification with women and masculine role relief, together with the weaker hypothesis of artistic expression. Prince used these four points to explain transvestism to at least one medical school class at the University of Southern California. Some of the students politely noted that the naming of these four points could not be a full explanation as no consideration was given to how they may have originated (from review of tape recording of Prince lecture, believed to be 1961).

## *Importance of the Girl Within*

Here are some comments concerning the girl within theory that I hope will help to put this valuable concept into a broader frame of reference. The key points are that the girl within is tantamount to the vague but essential concept of gender identity, and despite what Virginia had to say about the social construction of gender identity, at base, her girl within was determined by biology.

1. Prince postulates an inadequately defined group of feminine "potentials, possibilities, behaviors and yearnings" within "every male" that remain silent and unrecognized until brought forth by some "special event" that is a cross dressing experience. Put into the language of today's cognitive psychologists, all of this would be considered a *schema*, meaning a set of beliefs, predispositions, attitudes, and readiness for action, whether recognized at a conscious level or not. More important, were Prince writing today, perhaps she would allude to on-going studies of brain structures in the hypothalamus that have been shown, in animals, to be associated with sexual behavior and with changes in the developing brain, based on hormonal events during fetal development (For example, Diamond, 1965; Gorski, 1987; Hoenig, 1985). These studies raise the question of whether, in humans, there may be hormonal determinants *in utero* leading to brain structures that support both masculine and feminine gender identity and gender behavior. Hence, the rather unclear notion of a girl within may come down to individual differences in how the developing brain was influenced by hormones, or the capacity to respond to different hormones, during fetal development. For sex and gender researchers, the idea of a "girl within" is subsumed under the highly important concept of gender identity – one's perception of one's self relative to the dimensions of masculinity and femininity. While the possible biological roots of gender identity remain to be fully understood in humans, it seems clear that Valenti and Prince struck gold with their conception of a girl within. While their terminology may seem quaint or even simplistic, the essence of the concept is powerful and fits nicely with the current emphasis on the brain as the locus of the very human capability of experiencing a gender identity.

2. Prince postulates that the experience of "making contact" with one's girl within is an inherently pleasurable "...and exciting, exhilarating experience...not easily set aside." This recognition of the intense, powerful pleasure associated with cross dressing as almost universally reported by male cross dressers is of great importance. Very commonly, cross dressers describe this pleasure as an erotic experience that often is linked to masturbation and orgasm, although this is not universal. The main point here is that Virginia gave emphasis to the pleasurable affective rewards associated with cross dressing at a time when some mental health experts considered it pathological. Her tendency, however, has always been to more strongly emphasize the intellectual, rational, and logical aspects of cross dressing compared to the "feel good" or emotional aspects. In part, this may reflect her personality which is far more directed toward intellectualization than toward emotional expression. Many motivational theorists today would seek to become more explicit about the intense pleasure of cross dressing. No doubt, some would choose to focus on the role of neurotransmitters, such as serotonin, known to play a part in our affective or emotional experience. Others might give emphasis to the limbic system and other brain structures known to play important roles in both the experience of pleasure and in sexual arousal.

3. It is Prince's inclination, throughout her writing and into the present, to give greater weight to learning variables and other environmental factors compared to biological variables. In contrast, the trend over the past half century among sex and gender researchers trying to understand transvestism and transsexualism has been toward giving ever-greater

prominence to biological causation rather than to learning processes.

4. The special cross dressing event said to open up the opportunities for more complete expression of the male's "humanness" (that is, one's expression of his feminine inclinations and needs) is described as a simple learning or conditioning experience in which cross dressing is paired with a unique new understanding of the many feminine potentials and pleasures that were previously unrecognized. Prince does little to deal with the question of why some men who participate in such a special cross dressing events may not proceed to become cross dressers, although she recognized this as a problem. Prince does not account for what special characteristics the potential transvestite may have that are not seen in the male who experiences early cross dressing events but who does not become a cross dresser. Of course, nor has anyone else accounted for this. Robert Stoller believed that the critical event involved the male youth being cross dressed by a woman, thereby inducing both erotic excitement and intense humiliation (1985). He then reasoned that subsequent cross dressing was a highly erotic way to gain mastery over this sense of humiliation. A very different hypothesis would be that the future transvestite is neurologically predisposed to develop, first a masculine gender identity, and then in parallel, an ever-strengthening feminine gender identity. In a small percentage of transvestites, according to this reasoning, those having the most intense feminine gender identity may be motivated not only to develop exceptional skills in taking the gender role of a woman, but they also may ultimately come to live entirely as women and feel highly satisfied in this role. In fact, it is clear that such gender role reversals do occur in men who have lived for decades as what appeared to be typical heterosexual

transvestites. Prince's own history is an example of such a gender transformation.

5. Surprisingly, Prince gives only passing attention to the extensive research literature on the fascinating complexities of the intersex persons (Dreger, 1998); Ellis, 1945) or the studies of Money and Ehrhardt (1972), all of which raise major questions about the origins of gender identity. Prince is well aware of this literature and has come to know many of the researchers but she finds little application for these lines of study. Prince strongly leans on the idea of a self-concept that is capable of incorporating new or modified self perceptions concerning one's gender identity, but offers little to help us understand why men appear to differ greatly in their experience of having a feminine gender identity. Taken as a whole, Prince deserves much credit for her early recognition of the importance of the self system as a central component in transgender behavior.

# CHAPTER 12

# Battles with the Postal Authorities

We shall not attempt to explore the extensive history of how our Post Office managed to use its own regulations together with laws passed by the United States Congress to regulate sexual content delivered by mail. As late as the mid-1960s the so-called postal inspection process was much concerned with stopping the distribution of mail they considered pornographic or obscene. While no one knows to what extent they may have failed or succeeded to discover sexually offensive (to the inspectors) material, it is clear that they had considerable impact if only by putting everyone on notice that they would take a "pornographer" to federal court and press very serious charges. Virginia Price became a victim of this federal over-protection of the nation's mails. Here's what happened.

In the later part of 1959 a friend of Virginia's gave her the name and address of a person said to be a female who enjoyed corresponding with a cross dresser. Virginia's friend had met this individual through an advertisement concerning female impersonation that had run in a contact magazine. The invitation to write this so-called woman followed some sort of unpleasantness between the two original correspondents. Prince wrote explaining that he was a transvestite. In a 1962 conversation with Robert Stoller, she explained it this way: "Now, this woman had sent some pictures of two women fooling around with each other labeled "Me and You", and she had said several times in her letters, "ask me anything you want...I'll answer." Continuing with Stoller, "When I wrote to this girl who was purportedly a lesbian, I wrote a lesbian-type letter...It was a very stupid thing to do." The letter described what might be done sexually if the two "women" were to meet. Why might Virginia's letters to this person, who turned out to be another male cross dresser, be opened and read by the authorities? The answer is that Virginia's east coast correspondent was being monitored by the postal inspectors, and Virginia's letter was not only opened, but it was assessed as obscene.

When two postal inspectors first called upon Virginia (that is, as Arnold) they were friendly, but within days they had switched into their "bad guy" roles and hauled Arnold off to a federal office building, threatening him with serious prosecution and a possible prison sentence. Prince was out on bail within hours. The inspectors were persistent and they subsequently obtained an indictment charging Prince with mailing obscene material. When the case came to trial in federal court in February 1961, Virginia faced the possibility of a substantial prison sentence. Her attorney advised a plea of guilty to a lesser charge with no jail time, but with a five year probation period in which she must not use the mails "improperly" and during which she must not cross dress. Virginia agreed to these terms. Although the postal authorities also sought to end the publication of the newly established Transvestia magazine, the court did not order this. Prince never served any time in jail.

Before long, Virginia's attorney presented a suggestion to the sentencing judge to overcome the preclusion of her being cross dressed. The judge was asked to allow Virginia to cross dress while making educational presentations to service clubs, colleges, or church groups. All parties agreed that this was acceptable, and the attorney arranged for the first such luncheon talk to be given at his own Kiwanis Club in Alhambra. The main themes of these talks stressed the heterosexual basis of cross dressing contrasted with homosexual female impersonators and so-called drag queens, the difference between sex and gender, the harmlessness of cross dressing except as this impacts one's family, and the need for changes in public policy that discriminate or criminalize transvestism. Prince began these presentations long before the many television programs portraying cross dressers and transsexuals were on the air, and she was an immediate hit. Many invitations to speak to service clubs were received, and Virginia served as a very effective advocate for her views.

The growth of the civil rights movement in the 1960s, punctuated by the Stonewall Riot in New York City in 1969, led to civil rights initiatives that progressively diminished the power of postal inspectors to censor so-called pornographic material. In 1962, Prince called upon high-level postal officials in Washington, D. C., pleading her case with at least limited support, then met with the judge who had sentenced her. She convinced him that her probation should end. Virginia's career as a federal offender had ended.

In the 1960s, Prince began to seek opportunities for radio and television appearances, interviews with newspaper writers, meetings with police officials, and sessions with medical personnel throughout the United States. Often these presentations were arranged through the efforts of one of the members of a Tri Ess chapter. Her mission was to serve as the mouthpiece and missionary voice of the transgender movement. Her sword was the truth as she understood it, and her attraction was the rational and thoughtfully presented overview of her own life. More than anything else, Prince pleaded for public understanding of transgender behavior, and for a more fair appraisal of the harmlessness of such conduct. This is what sociologists would describe as attempts to "normalize" unusual behavior so as to encourage it to be viewed as more socially acceptable. It would seem difficult for the average citizen to see Virginia on television or hear one of her radio broadcasts and conclude that she was dangerous to anyone. These broadcasts and interviews with professionals were the first of their kind so far as transgender behavior is concerned.

Beginning in 1952, Christine Jorgensen had awakened the world to transsexual reassignment through surgery. Soon thereafter the concept of transsexualism became part of our language and one of the subdivisions of how sexual variations are classified in our culture (Meyerowitz, 2002). Prince, however, promoted the theme that no kind of surgery could produce a female. Her goal, therefore, was always to "...be the best woman I could possibly be..." without re-assignment surgery. The significance of her personal efforts to change laws, regulations, police tactics, or even the beliefs of psychiatrists may be debated, but what is clear is that Virginia Prince was a dynamic, persistent, and articulate role model for other transgender civil rights advocates. Her initiatives were sometimes imitated, but the scope and motivational drive to tell her story were unmatched.

# CHAPTER 13

# Three Motivational Themes

It is risky for a psychologist to believe he or she has any special credentials for examining the life of someone else, or even his own life. We are all inclined to give over-emphasis to some dimensions while failing to understand others. At worst, we can get it all wrong. At best, we can participate in just scratching the surface. In seeking a better understanding of the personality of Virginia Prince, I believe the following three major themes are the most important. As we review these, it is important to note that each of these themes runs into major conflict with each of the others.

## 1: A predisposition for feminine gender identity.

In my view, the most important motive that set the trajectory for Virginia's entire life was a predisposition to experience a strong sense of feminine gender identity. Having asserted this, my language could just as well be put into the words of Virginia Prince, who would say she was born with a powerful "girl within" – that is, a set of potentials for experiencing femininity that ultimately came into conscious awareness through her early cross dressing practices. As previously argued, perhaps this propensity is biologically "built in" to the central nervous system, possibly as a result of how the sex determining hormonal environment unfolds *in utero*. Virginia would reason that while some biological cause cannot be ruled out, it is mostly the product of extensive social learning. Her own history seems to support this point of view. Let's review Arnold's progression from being a fetishistic cross dresser to becoming a transgender woman.

### Step a: From fetishistic cross dresser to being a transgender woman.

As a teenage fetishistic cross dresser, while motivated to practice and gradually "construct" the best feminine image she could, Virginia had some things going for her. She was shorter than the average male, and her build, while not diminutive, was relatively short for men. She told Dr. Stoller that as a young adult she was about 5'8" tall -- today she is 5'5". Throughout much of her life her weight was about 145 pounds. Her facial structure was far from the most feminine that one might see in males, but with some careful makeup and a suitable hair style, she was very passable, as was soon demonstrated in scores of public settings. As she grew older, however, some of her feminine skills and body language gave way to a more androgynous style. In her late fifties or early sixties she obtained a face lift which may have been helpful for a few years. Additionally, she had taken female hormones for about six years during her late forties.

As a youth, Virginia also had two other assets that were invaluable: time and secrecy. We may ask whether Virginia's earliest fetishist cross dressing could possibly have unfolded as it did were she to have continued living in a residential school. Returning home to begin the seventh grade provided both the time and other opportunities essential to becoming a fetishistic cross dresser. Her focus was on what she saw in the mirror, and she was striving to produce the image of a complete woman. As she has told us, her primary goal in those early years was to become the best looking woman that she possibly could be. The skills she developed enabled her to experiment with being in public settings as a teenage woman, much earlier than is reported by most cross dressers.

The mirror played a key role by providing her with information about her appearance, and in particular, her ever growing skill in shaping the body of a woman and clothing this body to produce a convincing female profile. This process seems to have unfolded, step-by-step over a period of months or possibly years; we don't know the exact time frame. It was only when Virginia perceived herself in her mirror to be an appropriate looking woman that she felt sufficiently courageous to go out in public. Thereafter, while the mirror remained important as a way of checking on herself and arousing herself erotically, it was the social feedback that meant so much to her and ever-strengthened her sense of feminine gender identity. She had been practicing her feminine role presentation in public for about eighteen years before adopting the name, Virginia Prince.

The process of using the so-called "reflected appraisals of others" (Cooley, 1902) has been a major explanatory idea in identity construction theory for a century. Basically, Cooley said this: As we display social behavior, such as Virginia did when going out cross dressed, we pay special attention to the "reflected appraisals of others" to gauge the social impact of our conduct; we then make a judgment about the social acceptability of our conduct based on this feedback. It is the power of the social group that is supreme in this formulation, and while Cooley was not especially concerned with the formation of gender identity, his model fits Prince's favored social construction explanation quite nicely. This was never more clearly shown than when she went to Hawaii for a week in the early 1960s, testing herself to see if being in the same hotel, the same dining room, and among the same people for a week, could be carried off in a convincing way. Virginia was entirely satisfied with her successes throughout this Hawaiian vacation. It will be remembered that she also conducted a test of her ability to be perceived as Virginia a few years later when she attended the nude sensitivity training group in Palm Springs. It was the social evidence that she could be "seen as Virginia" even while clearly having the body of a male that was so highly valued as proof of her ability to "be Virginia." One caution: Virginia and other cross dressers may sometimes erroneously conclude that they have fully passed as women, when in fact, their observers are simply relating to them as women to avoid social embarrassment by anyone.

### Step b: From being a woman in public to having the gender identity of a woman.

As Virginia set the bar higher and higher in efforts to pass as a woman, she continued to experience success. There were no disastrous social experiences when Virginia was trying her wings. Progressively, she relied less upon her self-judgments -- the reflections in her mirror -- relying instead upon the reactions of other people. She essentially said at that time: Since others do see me as Virginia, then there really is a Virginia, despite having the anatomy of a man. For example, one of her favorite dress shops had an open dressing room providing little or no privacy. On many occasions she went there and used the dressing room to try on dresses and to reveal her underwear to other female patrons. These outings were more in the form of social experiments than mere shopping trips. Virginia told Stoller she would prepare her cleavage, her lingerie, and even a Kotex pad so as to provide a convincing feminine appearance. It was being seen as a woman by several other women in the dressing room that gave her increased confidence in her social standing as a woman.

On some occasions Virginia described herself as feeling somewhat like a multiple personality, in which both Charles and Virginia were not only present, but they were both essential to an erotic experience. At other times, she played down the multiple personality idea. She described to Dr. Stoller the process we are discussing here, in which the initial emphasis on fetishistic, mostly sexual excitement, gradually gave way to the "incorporation of this girl that he sees in the mirror when he puts on a dress and a wig and the rest of it" (Stoller, #28, p. 8). As she put it, "…it has simply become a new gender thing, and now it's a satisfaction and a pleasure and not necessarily erotic" ( p. 8).

Virginia characterizes herself as a transgender woman, not as a surgically created woman, but she has never surrendered her capacity to examine herself through the eyes of a man. This is in sharp contrast to the insistence of many male to female transsexuals that they are, in fact, women and they have always been women, and that they supposedly never were "actually" a man.

Arnold, and later, Virginia, perceived women as a virtual stereotype of late nineteenth century male thinking. Women were to be virtuous and delicate, sexually attractive but not to be taken advantage of, far less powerful than men and therefore much in need of protection, love, caring, tenderness, affection, and above all, never to be erotically or sexually violated. While this Victorian profile was surely seen by Prince, there was one exception: Virginia strongly believed that the woman holds a kind of sexual super power over the erotically needful but ineffectual man. The woman was seen as always in the controlling and regulatory position; the man was the supplicant with no real control. Hence, an important part of acquiring the identity of a woman, for Virginia, included gaining a special sexual power, status, and control.

Not everyone who met Virginia thirty years ago came away with a uniformly positive view of her as a woman, although in general, she has never run into any difficulty in passing. The daughter of present-day transsexual Chris Howey wrote a book about her family and she included some impressions from an evening with her then-transvestite father at a Cleveland support group. It happened that Virginia Prince was the guest of honor. She (Howey, 2002) described Prince this way: *"Although she lived as a woman, she did little to hide the fact that she still had all her original plumbing in place. She came in the room without knocking, grabbed herself a napkin's worth of hors d'oeuvres, and flopped into a chair, legs fanned in a perfectly unladylike "V"* (p. 164). Similarly, Dr. Stoller dictated notes to himself describing Virginia as something less than model woman. Once he noted "…she sat there, legs apart, like a football coach." Viginia's own assessment of her appearance was much in contrast to this description. In 1984 she said: "It amuses me that I am a heck of a lot better looking than most women I see, which may be a conceited remark considering the fact that I am now 72, but when I look at some women in their sixties, some of them look like they are at death's door" (Stoller, #29, p.18).

## 2: Sexual rewards across the lifespan

There is extensive documentation from Prince's articles in Transvestia, from her interviews with me, and from her discussions with Dr. Stoller, establishing the connection between Prince's cross dressing experiences and sexual arousal and orgasm. These were probably the most intense in her early years as a transvestite, but they have not disappeared. As we've noted, her erotic history parallels the classical scenario described by nearly all transvestites, and for Virginia, erotic play became a major source of pleasure throughout her life. Beginning with a pair of her mother's high heeled shoes, the pre-adolescent Arnold swiftly learned to masturbate and enjoyed the subsequent orgasm. This was followed by a hasty clean up, followed by a heavy burden of guilt, followed by the self-inflicted promise never to do that again. Soon thereafter, Arnold repeated the same behavior, with progressive use of more and more feminine clothing, gradually creating the appearance of a fully dressed woman. Months passed while Virginia learned the joy of watching her gradual creation of this woman-in-the-mirror, invariably accompanied by erection, masturbation and orgasm. Virginia never touched her penis when masturbating. She was able to stimulate herself through body movements while the penis was tucked against her abdomen. To accomplish this she experimented with several devices including a shield of hard rubber, a foam pad, and a swath of cloth arranged to hold the penis against her abdomen in a lubricated condom. Much like foreplay, she could enjoy hours of erection and heightened sexual arousal prior to orgasm, and without ever using her hands. She attempted to go one step farther by fabricating a simulation of the female genitalia and then trying to interest a manufacturer in making such a product, but without success.

Her most powerful sexual stimuli were a combination of her imagination along with the mirror image of herself wearing sexy underpants, stockings, garters, and high heels. She did not find her breasts responsive to physical stimulation. Her orgasms were described as "...far more intense and far more long-lasting than they ever were in the male sense" (Stoller, #28, p. 15). She said: "First there is anticipation and waiting and then it finally comes out in a great exhausting experience, and then believe me, I am wiped out" (p. 15). For Virginia, none of this sexual arousal was exclusively fetishistic. She has long seen it as erotic arousal that taps into her self-perception of Virginia as a woman. Her sexual arousal is associated with the confirmation of her feminine identity, not simply with sexually stimulating clothing. She put it this way in 1984: "I'm beginning to think of myself as a female with a penis and not as a male with breasts, if you dig that" (Stoller, #29, p. 8). This fits closely with her admiration and envy of so-called shemales, to be described later. Continuing, in the same interview she went farther in clarifying a gradual shift in her gender identity: "This whole erotic experience is tending to make me feel more like a female, not a female with a penis, but a female with a clitoris, but it happens to be a rather big one" (p. 11). Continuing the same idea, she added, "My eroticism is alive and well...I'm transferring the significance of it, mentally, to the idea of being a female (without any surgery"

(p. 14). Later, Virginia would insist upon using the word, woman, rather than, female.

For several years, Virginia maintained a strong interest in dancing, both as a social outlet and as a way to test her attractiveness to men. In Transvestia, she occasionally wrote of being hit upon by men in some of the 1960s era dance pavillions of Los Angeles. One of her favorites was the Starlight Ballroom. She came to enjoy not only having men ask her to dance, but also in detecting their erection while dancing. Even when alone, Virginia would occasionally catch a sexy glance of herself in her mirror and think: "My God, is that really me?" (Stoller, #17, p. 18).

She explained to Dr. Stoller: "This is an attempt to weld fantasy to reality…I'm trying to make believable to myself what is unbelievable." A bit later she concludes: "…the escape across the (gender) boundary into the other gender seems to me the greatest escape there is…that's what transsexuals are attempting to do – to make that great escape" (Stoller, #17, p. 39). Prince wanted Dr. Stoller to realize that her gender change was motivated by a positive force, as in "…moving toward something better and different." This is a radically more positive outlook than the traditional "gender dysphoria" explanation for making a gender role change.

Prince said that since her earliest experiences with cross dressing, she had always become "…excited by the idea of getting dressed or seeing other people dressed, or imagining or reading about it…" (Stoller, #17, p. 5). Therefore, Virginia became a collector of photographs, magazines, stories, and newspaper reports about cross dressing. For example, she enjoys a special pleasure, even today, when she examines full color magazine layouts showing the beautiful woman above the waist with the penis below the waist, in so-called shemales.

Psychologists refer to an organized set of ideas and beliefs as a *cognitive schema*, and this is a perfect description of the erotic power of imagination Prince experiences from cross gender stimulation of all kinds. It is not simply the beautiful woman that is the emotional stimulus; it is knowledge that a male is actually portraying a beautiful woman. She told Stoller that while Virginia could laugh at a comedy drag act wherein burly motorcycle riders wear elegant lingerie and makeup, the response of humor was totally different from the erotic enjoyment she would feel had these fellows been attractive as female impersonators. Like many transvestites, Virginia's imagination ranged across many different erotic situations and encompassed one of the most familiar fantasy images enjoyed by cross dressers, the street prostitute. When in the right mood, Virginia could "hitch up my skirt...and carry out the fantasy of getting undressed and so forth and so on" (Stoller, #17, p. 8). Invariably, Prince perceived herself to be the woman in all of her sexual fantasy scenes. For her, as with many cross dressers, this fantasy experience proved to be the most reliable and the most often used form of sexual enjoyment. After her second divorce, Prince never dated women; the woman in the mirror was her partner.

She believed her enjoyable sexual interludes would have been impossible without her penis and she often emphasized this to Dr. Stoller. It was a key part of her rationale for strongly advising against transsexual surgery for all except a few applicants, such as those who had little or no sexual motivation. She believed that the loss of male hormones after castration would diminish or even eliminate the delightful sexual arousal and orgasm that she had enjoyed her entire life, and that prospective candidates for surgery should be aware of such a potential loss. This reasoning is central to her insistence that gender reassignment surgery is generally a poor idea. The difficulty with this reasoning is not that it is clearly wrong, but that there are many motives for seeking gender reassignment having nothing to do with sexual arousal. In this matter, she seems to have over-generalized from her own experience, giving little weight to the motivations of others.

The significance of this history of highly valued sexual arousal and orgasm is that it helped to sustain the development of a more confident, more feminine, and more passable Virginia Prince. Equally important, it was a major source of her erotic enjoyment throughout all of her adult life. Additionally, this sexual theme became one of the main motivational forces contributing to what Prince would call the social construction of Virginia. It was never sex alone, but rather, there was also the creation a beautiful and sexual woman who served as an erotic stimulus, usually as perceived by herself, and sometimes by others. She said: "I think the (erotic) fantasies are kind of a way of fortifying and reinforcing my own sense of myself as a woman..." (Stoller, #17, p. 13). In seeking to understand Prince, this is a very important declaration on her part, and it came up more than once in her discussions with Dr. Stoller.

As a transgender woman in her early seventies, Virginia gained hours of erotic satisfaction when "once or twice a week...something would set it off (i.e., sexual arousal) and I'd say, what the hell, why not? I've got to get it out of the way one way or another (so) I get myself all gussied up and go do my thing" (Stoller, #28, p. 12). These erotic sessions invariably involved wearing high heels and lingerie she found sexually arousing, using a mirror and "seeing a female reflection," and they invariably culminated in orgasm, a source of pleasure reminiscent of the teenage Arnold secretly masturbating in his bedroom. She described these sessions as "physically exhausting" and requiring time to rest up and regain her full strength the following day. At a more psychological level, she also typically inflicted upon herself some of the reproach, perhaps even some of the guilt that Arnold had experienced when he was a teenager. She explained that following an orgasm, she would ask herself why that had seemed so important, and why she needed to "waste my time on something so stupid." This self-reproach and invocation of the Protestant work ethic is often voiced in the Stoller interviews. For Virginia it is one thing to discuss with her psychiatrist the joy of sex, but after a long and sexy session before her mirror admiring her feminine reflections, and then having a stronger orgasm "...than I ever had as Charles" she gives herself the kind of scolding that her hard-working parents might have delivered.

## 3: Achievement strivings; feelings of inadequacy and struggles with self-esteem

Virginia is a person who tends to business, and who has spent only a small percentage of her daily life concerned with either sexual play or the improvement of her feminine persona. She told me that as she reflected upon her own life, she was most pleased with having "...had some organizational skills, shown leadership on behalf of cross dressers, and nurturing the younger leaders" among the transgender groups. An important part of her identity is that she is and she has been productive, constructive, and worthy of respect. Like each of her parents, Prince wanted to be an entrepreneur, a shaker and mover, an innovator and a person commanding the admiration and respect of others. If a little money could be earned along the way that would be fine, but making money was never one of her primary objectives. There is an unmistakable motive cutting through all of this hard work: Prince valued what the rest of us thought of her, but more than anything else, I believe she sought to live a life worthy of the respect and admiration of her father. For reasons we will never understand, he denied his son this respect.

There is extensive evidence from Prince's hundreds of hours of discussion with Dr. Stoller that as a child, Arnold felt rejected by his father and he also felt a sense of inadequacy among his peers. He said: "I didn't see myself as being outstanding in any particular way. Other guys were bigger or stronger, or of athletic importance, or they'd be President of the class. I always ended up being Treasurer. I was always part of the structure but I was never top dog. Not until I got to be President of our Sunday School class. I was scared purple but I think I did a good job." Continuing: "I am (now) seen as a very powerful woman...one who stands up, who doesn't take a back seat, who's assertive. I'm the epitome of assertiveness. This happens because Arnold was not. Arnold was inferior and was always trying to compensate in some fashion. As Virginia, I just don't take a back seat to anybody on anything." And later: "Arnold might have said something in the same way as Virginia, but Arnold wouldn't have impressed other people" (Stoller, #24 p. 27). Unfortunately, this assertiveness and self-confidence has often involved being seen as disruptive, making mountains out of mole-hills, and showing an insensitivity for the feelings of others.

There is also evidence that the youthful Arnold felt less than competitive socially, but this is very common in teenagers. In one of her many discussions about these feelings she told Stoller: "I sure didn't think I had anything that would turn girls on. I got along all right with the other fellows but I wasn't as big as they were, and that made me feel somewhat inadequate in various ways" (Stoller, #24, p. 8). Then, looking back to his high school days he added: "I wouldn't have had to feel inadequate if I had been a beautiful girl." Prince often expressed to Stoller the idea that even if Arnold had done something that deserved admiration and respect, that this would not have been properly recognized by his father or his peers. In contrast, Prince reasoned, had he grown up as a girl these outstanding qualities would have somehow been fully appreciated by others. Virginia felt that women simply are judged by different standards than men.

Looking back to Arnold's high school years, Virginia consistently plays down whatever accomplishments had been attained; there is a diminishment, an undercutting of the foundations of self esteem. Here's how she described it: "Arnold went into science and he went into track and field, except that I was small so I got on to the Class C team which was based on height and weight, not performance. I had to prove my adequacy even there. For some time I held the school record for the 660 (yard run) which is what the Class C students ran. I had to prove that I was some kind of man, even though I was a little squirt" (Stoller, #24, p. 10). His father's lack of interest in his athletic efforts must have been very hurtful to the high school age Arnold because he told Stoller

126

"Actually, my dad took less interest in me than I might reasonably have thought he should have..." (Stoller, #24, p. 14). At another time, Dr. Stoller had commented that "You weren't all that little, you weren't puny. It sounds like your father had some concern that you weren't manly enough" (Stoller, #24, p. 13).

If you were to join Virginia for lunch at the Be All You Can Be Weekend or at any of the many transgender conventions she likes to attend, you'd be impressed with something that nearly all of her friends have noted: Virginia is a very forceful and domineering talker. In social situations when she is in the role of the expert, she seems devoid of the conversational skills most people take for granted. Perhaps this autocratic and opinionated style of interaction, the tendency to discount opinions she does not favor, is mostly a façade masking a fear that she won't be taken seriously unless she is alone on the stage of life, playing her part and deserving top billing and all the applause. At least, that's the way she comes off when in the role of the expert. In more private settings, such as at lunch or in her own home, her style is far more conversational, thoughtful, and aware of the importance of being a listener.

At her retirement community, the residents assemble for dinner each evening, and many go out of their way to circulate among the various tables to visit with the elderly folks. Virginia soon tired of this somewhat demanding and unrewarding procedure. Instead, she fell into a habit of taking her tray to an alcove apart from the main dining area where she is sometimes joined by an elderly female attorney who also prefers to avoid most other guests. Prince is very aware that she is not fully understood or appreciated by many of the other residents, but she told me that this is something she simply does not care about. Apparently this is not an audience likely to give Virginia either the attention or the applause she would like to enjoy. Her tactic, instead, is to build close relationships with a small number of persons invited to join her for the discussion of abstruse topics involving theories of evolution, cosmology, or atomic physics. "The people here are trying to figure me out," she told me, "and so far they haven't been successful." Comments from two of her fellow residents revealed that Virginia is perceived as something of a peculiar and enigmatic individual who does not quite fit in.

For twenty years, Virginia devoted thousands of hours to the writing and editing of Transvestia with very modest financial returns. In the early years the publication barely broke even, and the mailing list never reached one thousand. Her initiative as the founder fit her need to see herself as a forceful, effective editor-publisher who could overcome all obstacles, and when necessary, even finance this struggling publication. The theme of needing to be productive, creative, and deserving of attention as an organizer-leader has not diminished much even as she passed her ninetieth birthday. At her retirement community she has continued to audit college courses at Pomona University, and to lead a discussion group concerned with cosmology and other topics of little interest to most of the guests.

Prince also has a need to be an unheralded patron of persons-in-need. For many years, she has contributed money on a regular basis to needful men and women, and she continues to do so. Undoubtedly, most of those she has attempted to assist have been both needy and deserving, but now and then she has been taken in by individuals seeking money and promising to repay substantial amounts handed out by the rather trusting Virginia. It doesn't require too much imagination to think of her, longing to imitate her generous and beloved father, Dr. Charles Lowman, who never turned away a child from his medical clinic or his Orthopedic Hospital. Prince's generosity has occasionally reflected a surprising lack of insight into the manipulations of others who sought a financial hand-out. Such persons, so far as I am aware, have typically not been affiliated with the transgender community. We may speculate that, at least in part, this motive to assist the underdog may have provided close relationships that have so seldom been a part of her life.

The stress and strain of living as a man with all of the cultural expectations that come with this role have received much attention from Virginia. In Transvestia articles and in the many hours we have spent together, she has emphasized the idea of escaping from the demands of the man's role in our culture as a major reason for cross dressing and also for becoming a woman. She has often used the analogy of "taking a vacation" from the masculine role. Perhaps this theme of escaping masculine role pressures is somehow connected with the more basic motivation to somehow please her unrewarding father, to earn his respect and approval, and to ultimately become the honored son, the Prince with shining armor, in the service of the king.

# CHAPTER 14

# Virginia at 90

At the age of 88 and living alone in her Hollywood canyon home, Virginia experienced a minor health problem that was not life-threatening, but it stimulated a desire to sell her home and move to a retirement community. She swiftly moved toward this goal, doing everything that needed to be done and actually moving within a year. Now, at the age of 90, she lives in a one-bedroom duplex on the grounds of an extensive retirement center in Claremont, California. This twenty acre layout includes separate detached homes, duplex units, apartments of all sizes, a central dining facility, and an assisted living center. Medical supervision of the guests is provided. The oldest resident is just over 100 years of age and the youngest is about 70. There are far more women than men. She still drives her 1993 Mercury on the Los Angeles freeways, and she frequently goes out to shop at stores and to visit professionals. She maintains a few nice friendships with other guests including one retired clinical psychologist and one sculptor, both of whom responded most pleasantly to her revelations concerning her transgender history.

Virginia always enjoyed a little gardening, and on the day I had approached her place she was snipping a cutting from one of the many vines framing her entryway. She gave this to the daughter of the elderly lady who used to live next door, but who required more care and was transferred to the assisted living center. I snapped a picture of Virginia, and then entered her living room -- a collection of well used furniture, papers of all kinds on every horizontal surface, boxes remaining in place since her move here two years ago, books, photographs, and a few small pieces of decorative art. Although part of her rent pays for housekeeping services, Virginia prefers to have her many papers and magazines distributed across several rooms in a disorganized fashion. In the corner is the electronic organ that she has not played for some time, and off in a small alcove is the computer given to her by a long-time friend. Propped against the wall, not far from the computer is a full-length mirror allowing her to check her appearance as she works on the most urgent mail, bills, and e-mail. The table is covered with several layers of books, magazines and envelopes as Virginia complains that she can't find the letter she intended to show me. Instead, she showed me the most recent bill indicating a monthly increase in the cost of staying at this residence, where she receives one meal per day. Fear not, she has her own stove and refrigerator and she does not go hungry.

She had dusted off a chair in the corner of the living room with a lamp overhead so I would be comfortable as we talked. Throughout the day I had been using a checklist to clarify some factual details of her life. We chatted as two good friends who know each other fairly well. Although it was the final day of January, the temperature in Claremont was breaking records at 91 degrees (F.). Virginia wanted me to know that some elements of her sex life had returned, at least in part. She happily reported that an especially gratifying sex video had not only produced something of an erection, but that some orgasmic sensations also occurred. One of her most favored videotape stimuli for sexual arousal has been the beautiful upper body and face of a sexy shemale; the pictures of the male genitalia, however, are considered, in her view, too sexually explicit. "I always 'fast-forward' the videotape during those parts," she explained.

Looking back across her life, Virginia commented that one small "disappointment" was that after getter her Ph.D. she "...really didn't make much use of it." I asked her if there were any major changes she would make in her life if she had the chance to do so: "Well...I guess that would involve the question of having reassignment surgery, but I don't think I'd have done that."

Moving on to another topic, Virginia exclaimed: "Oh, take a look at what my friend sent me," urges Virginia, handing me a Xerox copy of a one page black and white flyer. This showed a rather masculine appearing transgendered male with prominent breasts and decorative bikini-style underpants. Prince was obviously much intrigued with this picture. "I met this chap five years ago...he's also a highly trained scientist, and he has a nice wife and family," she explained. "But now he is using the internet to work as a shemale escort, having dates with men for sex, or taking shy cross dressers out for a night on the town." It was clear that Virginia was very interested in the accomplishments of her friend and that she wanted me to know that she also envied him. I stuck to my own agenda, knowing that she tends to swerve off the topic. However, twice again during the afternoon she diverted our conversation back to her shemale friend and urged me to again examine the pictorial advertisement. Speaking softly and with carefully chosen words, she wanted me to understand her fascination with the picture: "I know I'm envious of what he is doing...he is having sex as a woman, yet he is still anatomically a male, and he is able to do this with the apparent approval of his wife and family." There was a softer, slower, quality to Virginia's description; her eyes were locked onto the picture she had showed me. I inquired what she really intended by use of the word "envy." She explained it this way: "He can do all of this entirely as a woman...and yet he is actually a man, and he can do it without losing his loved ones." She seemed not only envious but also to feel a sense of sadness. Virginia Prince, after all, has suffered enormous losses of loving family relationships throughout her life, at least in part, due to her transgender behavior. It's fair to ask: Who did Virginia really love during her life, and who really loved Virginia? While comparing her life experiences and family problems to the life of the shemale, perhaps she was also considering the reality of being 90 and all that this implies. Her envy may have included not only admiration of the feminine body, but also the fact that when you're 90 you face an uncertain future, and your much prized cleavage isn't quite what it used to be.

We discussed a few more topics from my checklist -- the Los Angeles locations of her parent's homes and the two divorces, the formation of the early Tri Ess chapters, and then Virginia returned to something she had brought up at lunch: "Hey...would you like to see a little of the Wild Women "porno" videotape I told you about?" Sure, I said, putting my pen away. She fetched the videotape, for she was clearly weary of serious biographical analyses for this day. We then watched a $19.95 black and white video she'd bought by mail order showing teenage girls squirming and undulating at various stages of undress as the off-screen male voice gave directions: "Good...move to the left...perfect....more...that's fine, beautiful." It was part of a series filmed in Florida and fell considerably short of memorable cinema.

134

Virginia explained that for the past two years she has seldom experienced a real erection, possibly due to some of the medication she is taking for an enlarged prostate, "But that doesn't mean I can't enjoy watching these videos now and then...," she added. At 90, her capacity for erotic rewards may be different than in years past, but it has surely not disappeared. Within a few minutes I was bored and began thumbing through the pages of a recent edition of Transgender Tapestry. She turned off the videotape. It was getting late. I gathered my papers and stuffed them into a large manila envelope, signaling the end of my visit.

When I arrived that morning Virginia's makeup and hair were carefully done, and her blue-gray top and matching blue print skirt with beige stockings were fresh and trim. She appeared as a nicely turned out older lady ready for the day. We had spent the morning on a string of serious and very personal topics, and then enjoyed lunch in the community dining room. After lunch Virginia explained to the kitchen staff how some of the salad bar items might be better arranged, and especially, the importance of having the two different kinds of lettuce in separate containers. We had walked a few hundred yards back to her home and continued with my questions. But now it was four in the afternoon, and her makeup was faded, her hair needed a bit of attention, and she was growing weary. Sitting with her legs somewhat askew, smiling and joking about the sexy young girls in the "porno" video, it seemed to me that Virginia felt like taking a nap.

I got up and gave her a hug and offered my sincere thanks for her putting up with my interrogation. Moving across her front porch, I threaded my way between exercise equipment and her new, mini-mobile wheelchair that is seldom required. My car was nearby. "Drive carefully," she reminded me in a motherly, caring way. I gave her a smile and a wave as I started to drive up the tree lined campus of this spacious and attractive college-like facility, and I said to myself: Virginia is one Good Samaritan who has been traveling down the road of life, doing what she can to assist those in need, tending to business, and staying focused on her life-mission. She is still moving ahead, still taking an active part in every group she belongs to, still upbeat and full of ideas, and she is a transgender pioneer who has earned a lot of respect for all she has contributed to the transgender movement. Thank you, Virginia.

# REFERENCES

Buckner, H. T. (1970). The transvestite career path. *Psychiatry, 33,* 381-389.

Bullough, V. L. & Bullough, B. (1993). *Cross dressing, sex, and gender.* Philadelphia: University of Pennsylvania Press.

Cooley, C. H. (1902). *Human nature and the social order.* New York: Scribner.

Diamond, M. (1965). A critical evaluation of the ontogeny of human sexual behavior. *Quarterly Review of Biology, 48,* 147-175.

Dreger, A. D. (1998). *Hermaphrodites and the medical invention of sex.* Cambridge, MA: Harvard University Press.

Ellis, A. (1945). The sexual psychology of human hermaphrodites. *Psychosomatic Medicine, 7,* 108-125.

Ellis, H. (1928). *Eonism and other supplementary studies.* Philadelphia: F. A. Davis.

Gagnon, J. H. & Simon, W. (1973). *Sexual conduct: The social sources of human sexuality.* Chicago: Aldine.

Gorski, R. A. (1987). Sex differences in the rodent brain: Their nature and origin. In: Reinisch, J. M., Rosenbloom, L. A., & Sanders, S. A. (Eds.*), Masculinity/Femininity: Basic perspectives.* (pp. 37-67). New York: Oxford University Press.

Hamburger, C, Sturup, G. K. & Dahl-Iversen, E. (1953).
Transvestism: Hormonal, psychiatric, and surgical treatment.
*Journal of the American Medical Association, 152,* 391-396.

Hirschfeld, M. (1910). *Die Transvestiten.* Leipzig: Max Spohr.
English translation: Lombardi-Nash, M (1991). *Transvestites:
The erotic drive to cross dress.* New York: Prometheus Books.

Hoenig, J. (1985). The origin of gender identity. In: Steiner, B.
W. (Ed.), *Gender dysphoria: Development, research and
management.* (pp. 11-29). New York: Plenum Press.

Meyerowitz, J. (2002). *How sex changed: A history of
transsexuality in the United States.* Cambridge, MA: Harvard
University Press.

Money, J. & Ehrhardt, A. (1972). *Man and woman, boy and
girl: The differentiation and dimorphism of gender identity
from conception to maturity.* Baltimore, MD: Johns Hopkins
University Press.

Prince, V. (c. 1961). *An Introduction to the subject of
transvestism, or femmiphilia (cross dressing)* (parentheses in
the original title), printed privately.

Prince, V. (1976). *Understanding cross dressing.* Los Angeles:
Chevalier Publications.

Prince, V. (1980). *Transvestia,* Vol. 100. Los Angeles:
Chevalier Publications.

Prince, V. & Bentler, P. M. (1972). Survey of 504 cases of
transvestism. *Psychological Reports, 31,* 903-917.

Stoller, R. J., (1985). *Presentations of gender.* New Haven: Yale University Press.

# INDEX

## A

Alpha Chapter, v, xiii, 41, 55, 56, 58, 89, 90, 94

## B

Be All You Can Be Weekend, 94, 132
Beaumont Society, 97
Beecroft, Carol, 87, 96
Bentler, Peter, 82
Bindrim, Paul, 58
Boswell, Holly, 96
Bowman, Karl, 50
Bruce, Virginia, ix, xiii, 70, 74
Buckner, H. T., 83
Bullough, Bonnie, v, 55
Bullough, Vern, v, viii, 5, 40, 66, 149
Burchert, Eve, 96

## C

California State University, Northridge, v, vi, 5, 62, 81, 87
Cardinal Industries, 2, 37, 43, 81
CHIC, 90
cognitive schema, 127
Cook-Riley, Yvonne, 96

## D

dancing, 73, 126
Diagnostic and Statistical Manual, ix
divorce, 13, 16, 32, 33, 39, 43, 52, 66, 127
Docter, Shirley Long, vii

## E

editor, 62, 780, 85, 93, 133
Ellis, Havelock, ix
Ellis, Irene, v
entrepreneur, 130
envy, 21, 22, 72, 125, 140
eonism, ix

141

explain transvestism, 106, 108

# F

Fairfax, Jane and Mary, 87
Fantasia Fair, 95
Fee, Jane, v, 96, 98, 100
female hormones, 52, 119
feminine appearance, 122
feminine mannerisms, 72
Femme Mirror, 87
femmiphile, 107
fetal development, 109
fetishism, x, 46, 57, 71, 150
fetishistic cross dresser, 6, 119, 120
First Congregational Church, 5
first presentation, 48
Foundation for Full Personality Expression, 55, 93
FPE, 55, 89, 93, 97
Frye, Phyllis Randolph, 96, 100

# G

Gagnon, John, x
Gardner, Tony, vi
gender dysphoria, 126
gender identity, x, 47, 48, 54, 59, 63, 101, 109, 111, 112, 118, 120, 121, 125, 144
gender role, xiii, 50, 104, 112, 126
girl within, 7, 47, 63, 101, 102, 103, 104, 108, 109, 110, 118
Glendora Foothill School, 25
Good Samaritan Hospital, 6
Green, Jamison, 96

# H

Halloween, 48
Hamburger, Christian, x
high heeled shoes, 45, 55, 83, 124
Hijras, ix
Hirschfeld, Magnus, ix
Hoff, Joan, vi

homosexual feelings, 42, 74
Hose and Heels Club, 55
Howey, Chris, 123

## J

John Burroughs Junior High School, 26
Jorgensen, Christine, x, 29, 72, 116

## K

Kabuki, ix
Kane, Ariadne, 95, 96
Kinsey Institute, 81
Kirk, Sheila, 96

Kiwanis Club, 115

## L

Laing, Alison, vi
Laing, Dottie, vi, 96
lingerie, 15, 47, 122, 127, 129
Lowman, Arnold ix, xiii, 5, 6, 13, 28, 31, 32, 34, 39, 58
Lowman, Brent, 2, 3, 32, 34, 36, 42, 43, 52, 56
Lowman, Elizabeth, 21
Lynd, Betty Ann, 96
Lynn, Merrissa Sherrill, 95, 96
Lawrence, Louise, 29, 49, 81, 86
Los Angeles High School, 26

## M

Mamselle, 87
masculine role, 105, 108, 134
masturbation, x, 34, 45, 47, 70, 84, 105, 110, 124
Mattachine Society, 54
Miller, Niela, vi, 149
mirror, 22, 46, 63, 120, 121, 122, 124, 125, 126, 127, 129, 138
Money, John, 102
Muriel, 1, 45, 50, 79

**N**

neurotransmitters, 110
New York City, 81, 85, 86, 115
nude session, 59

**O**

obscene, 3, 8, 84, 113, 114
orgasm, 45, 47, 52, 63, 105, 110, 124, 128, 129
Orthopedic Hospital, 9, 10, 11, 12, 18, 20, 134
Oviatt Library, 81
Owen, Naomi, 94, 96

**P**

Palladium, 11, 73
Palm Springs, 58, 60, 121
persons-in-need, 134
Pomona College, 1, 26, 27, 28
pornographic, 84, 113, 115
postal authorities, 70, 84, 114
Prince, Charles, ix, xiii
Prince-Stoller interviews, xiii, 65
Prince-Stoller transcripts, vii
prostitute, (Virginia as) 127
psychoanalytic, 67
purposes of Transvestia, 79

**R**

reflected appraisals, 120
rewards of cross dressing, 70
Richard Green, 66
Richard Smith, v, viii, 5
Rikki Swin, vi, 87
Robert Stoller, vi, 3, 4, 7, 12, 17, 20, 39, 65, 74, 111, 113

**S**

San Diego, 56
San Francisco, 2, 10, 15, 27, 28, 39, 41, 49, 50, 51, 53, 72
self esteem, 131
self-reproach, 129

sex change, 72
sexual excitement, 47, 122
shemale, 125, 127, 139
Shepherd, Clara, 35
Shepherd, Dorothy, 28, 31
Sherry, 41, 74
Simon, William, x
Sister Mary Elizabeth, 96, 100
Skinner, Doreen, 3, 38, 52
SRS, 61
Stanford University, 62
Stoller transcripts, 50, 67
Stonewall, 81, 115
Summers, Ellen, 96
Superior Court, 34

## T

Terminology, xiii
Thomas, Sandy, v, 62, 87, 90, 151
Thorn, Johnny, 54, 78
Transgender era, 57
Transgender movement, ix
transgender woman, 49, 62, 119, 122, 129
transgenderism, (definition) xiii
transvestism and cross dressing, xiii
Tri Ess, 55, 77, 87, 89, 93, 94, 95, 96, 97, 116

## U

UCLA Neuropsychiatric Institute, 65
Ultralite aircraft, 60
University of California Medical Center, 27
University of Southern California, 9, 65, 108

## V

Valenti, Susanna, 85, 86, 101,    102
Viagra, 63
Volkovskis, Valdis, vi

## W

Walworth, Janis, vi, 60
Wilcox, Barbara Ann, 29